Everything on a Waffle

Everything on a Waffle

a Waffle

Polly Horvath

SCHOLASTIC INC.
New York Toronto London Auckland Sydney
Mexico City New Delhi Hong Kong Buenos Aires

Author's note
Although Coal Harbour is a real place,
I've changed the geography of it
to suit my story.

ISBN 0-439-44039-4

12 11 10 9 8   3 4 5 6 7/0

Printed in the U.S.A.   23

First Scholastic printing, September 2002

Designed by Abby Kagan

For Jay

Contents

My Parents Are Lost at Sea   3

I Move to Uncle Jack's   14

The Dead Whalers   20

I Am Almost Incarcerated   31

Lena's Boiled Potatoes   38

What Miss Bowzer Knew   48

I Lose All My Sweaters   58

I Lose a Toe   65

Uncle Jack's Idea   81

I Set Fire to a Guinea Pig   88

Dinner at The Girl on the Red Swing   97

I Lose Another Digit   108

Fire!   118

Miss Perfidy Leaves   125

Everybody Goes Home   140

Everything on a Waffle

My Parents Are Lost at Sea

I live in Coal Harbour, British Columbia. I have never lived anyplace else. My name is Primrose Squarp. I am eleven years old. I have hair the color of carrots in an apricot glaze (recipe to follow), skin fair and clear where it isn't freckled, and eyes like summer storms.

One June day a typhoon arose at sea that blew the rain practically perpendicular to our house. My father's fishing boat was late getting in and my mother, who wasn't one for sitting around biting her nails, put on her yellow macintosh and hat and took me over to Miss Perfidy's house, saying, "Miss Perfidy, John is out there somewhere and I don't know if his boat is coming safely into shore, so I am going out in our sailboat to find him." Well, a thinking person might have told my mother that if a big fishing boat wasn't going to make it through those waves, our little skiff sure wasn't. But

Miss Perfidy wasn't one to waste time in idle chitchat. She just nodded. And that was the last I saw of my mother.

The fishing boat never came back to shore. Neither did the skiff. So all that June I continued to live with Miss Perfidy. There was a memorial service for my parents but I wouldn't go. I knew that my parents hadn't drowned. I suspected that they had washed up on an island somewhere and were waiting to be rescued. Every morning I went down to the docks to watch the boats come in, sure that I would see my parents towed in, perhaps on the back of a whale.

"I don't know what you think the story of Jonah is about, Miss Perfidy," I said. "But to me it is about how hopeful the human heart is. I am certain my parents, if not in the belly of a whale, are wondering how I am doing and trying to get home to me!" I called the last few words out in the direction Miss Perfidy had gone. She often stalked off when I was in the middle of a sentence. It didn't encourage many heartfelt confidences.

I didn't mind Miss Perfidy's exits, but what I did mind was her mothball smell, which was never overwhelming yet hovered around her in a little fog. Mothballs spilled from every drawer in her house. I couldn't understand why Miss Perfidy seemed to be the only person in town who had such a huge problem with moths. One day I got out a box and read the directions. "You know, Miss Perfidy," I said, "is it possible that you misunderstood the directions? You seem to be using an awful *lot* of mothballs." But Miss Perfidy had already left the room.

Besides, it wasn't really any of my business. The town council was paying Miss Perfidy her usual baby-sitting fee of three dollars an hour from what they called the Squarps' estate and what I called my parents' bank account until they could figure out what to do with me. This was taking them a lot longer than it might have because my parents hadn't made wills or thought ahead to the day when they would both disappear at sea. But even I knew that at three dollars an hour I wasn't long for life with Miss Perfidy.

One member of the town council argued that three dollars an hour was a lot to pay a baby-sitter for those endless night hours when I was asleep and Miss Perfidy was snoring in her own bed, but it was fruitless to argue with Miss Perfidy. She was mean with money. In Coal Harbour there was whaling and fishing and the navy. If you didn't whale or fish or do naval things you had to do what you could to hold body and soul together, so Miss Perfidy was tight with her pennies by necessity. When things had gotten too tight a few years back she had sold her small cottage and bought an even smaller cottage. Before she moved from the small cottage she dug up her flower bulbs one by one—tulips, daffodils, crocuses—and not being a real stinker, neatly filled in all the holes again. When the realtor heard about it, he came charging over. "Miss Perfidy," he had said. "You just can't do this. People expect you to *leave* your flowers." But she said she had paid for and planted every last bulb and she was taking every last bulb, and speaking of bulbs she was also unscrewing and taking all the lightbulbs. Land's sakes, did he want her to leave her clothes for the new owners too?

Toward the beginning of August, when the town council finally decided to invite me to a meeting to discuss my fate, they sent Miss Honeycut, the school guidance counselor, to escort me and Miss Perfidy. Miss Honeycut was the closest thing Coal Harbour had to a psychiatrist, which wasn't really very close at all. Everyone knew that Miss Honeycut was born to the British aristocracy and was going to inherit half of Yorkshire, England, when her father, still kicking around at eighty-three, died. People were very, very nice to her because they thought that maybe someday she would remember them in her will. Or at least invite them to visit her manor house in Yorkshire when she finally got her mitts on it. Only my mother had avoided Miss Honeycut. She said that despite Miss Honeycut's vast global experience, she was a bore. That she talked exclusively in anecdotes and couldn't converse like normal people and that the reason she was stuck way across the world in Coal Harbour was that it was the only place she could get a job and *that* because her father knew the principal of Coal Harbour Elementary.

But I wished I could hear more about the places Miss Honeycut had traveled and the things she had seen. I remember her telling my mother that as a little girl she had learned to play bridge riding a train through China. It didn't seem fair that when she was my age she had already learned more about the world than perhaps I would ever have the chance to.

When Miss Honeycut came to the door, Miss Perfidy and I were ready. Miss Perfidy was wearing a very old tweed suit and carrying a black patent leather handbag over her forearm. Miss Perfidy knew that no one would want to tussle with someone in such a Queen of England getup and that this gave her the upper hand. She was never happy unless she had the upper hand. Unfortunately, neither was Miss Honeycut and she looked at Miss Perfidy as if a tuna fish had just died on her foot.

All the way to the meeting Miss Honeycut kept saying how sorry she was that my parents had died, and she said "died" in a very pointed way until I finally explained that she must be mistaken and I was content to wait for my parents' return no matter how long it took. Miss Honeycut said that this was a most unrealistic attitude and that I must think of my future. Miss Perfidy didn't say anything the whole way there but sniffed disapprovingly at both of us.

In the meeting hall we took seats near the front, waiting for more people to drift in. Miss Perfidy continued to sniff. She sniffed so heartily people in rows forward and back of her began sniffing to detect what Miss Perfidy smelled. Soon nearly everyone was sniffing.

"They've all got colds," grumbled Miss Perfidy, turning to look accusingly at me. "Big crowd packed into a small hall. We're all going to get sick now."

I didn't know what to say, so I looked at my feet, then got out my mother's memo pad, which I kept in my back pocket. It had fallen out of my mother's raincoat when she left me at Miss Perfidy's. There wasn't much in there, just her recipe for carrots in an apricot glaze and an old grocery list. The rest of the pages were blank. I read and reread the recipe as we sat waiting for the meeting to start.

When the last person had drifted in and had a sniff, Miss Honeycut started the meeting by saying that my parents' bank account was dwindling and, as imperfect an arrangement as she thought it might be to have me move in with a relative I didn't even know, the town council must try to summon my next of kin, Mr. Jack Dion, because, after all this time, he was the only kin they could find any reference to and no one else was volunteering to take me in.

Well, good luck to you, I thought because the one time my mother had mentioned Uncle Jack, her brother, to me, she had said he was a drifter. "Old hotfoot Jack" she called him. Miss Honeycut had found out that he was in the navy now, stationed all the way across the country in Halifax, Nova Scotia.

I figured it would be a miracle if he ended up in Coal Harbour, but that's exactly what did happen. After the meeting, the council contacted Uncle Jack at sea and he said he couldn't come, but immediately after that, the navy shifted everyone around and he got shifted right onto the base in Coal Harbour, which the town council thought was very fortuitous as he could take care of this mess, by which they meant me.

As soon as Uncle Jack arrived, he was whisked off to a town council meeting. When Uncle Jack, who was tall, mustached, broad-shouldered, blond, and ruddy, walked into the room, Miss Honeycut eyed him thoughtfully. This surprised me because Uncle Jack looked like a pig, albeit a lean, *good-looking* pig, whereas Miss Honeycut looked more like a turtle. It was hard to imagine a pig and a turtle together but it gave me something to do through the rest of the meeting.

The council reminded Uncle Jack that I was still hanging out at Miss Perfidy's waiting to be claimed and costing three dollars an hour. Uncle Jack seemed confused when they told him this. He had assumed that when he said no, the town council had found some other relative or guardian for me. He explained that he was a training officer and had just moved into a small house connected to the gym on the base. It was very convenient for him because he taught classes in the gym and worked out there every day but he wouldn't be allowed to keep a child there. If he wanted to do that, he would have to move to the family housing part of the base. And he really didn't want to do that. The town council looked horrified when he told them this. They had wanted him to go all gooey when he saw me. I didn't. I admired his honesty. After all, we both had lives already in gear.

The meeting dragged on and on because as usual there were three people who loved to hear themselves talk and wouldn't shut up and it took the moderator a long time to figure out that none of them had anything to say. They exhausted everyone so much that the most that could be decided was that Uncle Jack should think about things, and they left it at that. Everyone broke for cake and coffee.

Miss Honeycut noodled her way up to Uncle Jack with an extra piece of cake. What he was supposed to do with it I didn't know because he already had a piece on his plate and another jammed up his cheek. Since I had finished my piece, I said I'd take it. Miss Honeycut gave me a look. She handed me the cake, though, since Uncle Jack was watching. Then Miss Honeycut started telling Uncle Jack that she never thought he should have been asked to take a child on. How she felt it was an awful imposition for a bachelor, relative or no, ho ho ho. How he needn't feel badly about not being up to the challenge. Uncle Jack looked at her coolly when she said this. Miss Honeycut went on swiftly—an officer's job was challenging enough. She knew. Her father had been an officer. It was such a startling about-face position that I stood with my mouth hanging slightly open, full of half-eaten cake. Miss Honeycut went on to say how there were many excellent foster homes for children like me and people did, despite what you heard, frequently adopt the older child, and that's when Uncle Jack put his arm around me and said he had decided to take care of me himself. It was a nice warm hug and the first real human contact I had had since this whole business began. And it was comforting, even though I knew he had only done it to spite Miss Honeycut.

"Don't worry," I said to Uncle Jack later on, "I don't expect it will be for long. I'm sure my mother and father will be here anytime now."

Then the navy sent its Coal Harbour troops on a peacekeeping mission and announced the government's decision to close down the base permanently. The town thought Uncle Jack was going too and they were back to square one. That's when he surprised everyone by quitting the navy, getting into real estate, and buying the house connected to the gym on the base. It was, he said, a good deal because he got the gym thrown in for free. He really loved that gym.

And so I ended up with my clothes and things in three houses: the house that Uncle Jack bought, Miss Perfidy's house, where I continued to keep the sweaters that my mom had knit for me so they would be moth-free, and my own house, which Uncle Jack put up for rent. It sent me deeper into a funny, detached, dreamlike state. I do not live anywhere anymore, I said to myself on one of my walks down to the pier to wait for my parents. I am not in the body of life. I hover on the extremities. I float.

Carrots in an Apricot Glaze

Take a package of carrots and scrape them. Chop the carrots into bite-sized pieces. Open a tin of apricots. Save them for something else and pour the juice into the pan with the carrots and a little water. Add 2 tablespoons of butter and 3 tablespoons of brown sugar—more if you like them sweeter, less if you don't. Boil them until the carrots are tender, adding water if the liquid starts to disappear and a glaze appears before the carrots are cooked. The liquid should boil down and turn into a glaze just as the carrots become tender.

I Move to Uncle Jack's

Through the rest of the summer I continued to float. Uncle Jack asked me if I minded moving but I could not shake the sense that none of it mattered very much.

"Well," I said to Miss Perfidy as Uncle Jack helped me to carry my things to his car, "I guess this is . . ." but she left the room as soon as Uncle Jack was out the door, so I was muttering goodbye to an empty room.

When school started, my real troubles began. Miss Honeycut had taken children out of the classroom in groups to counsel them about my bereavement. I wasn't supposed to know about this but I found out one day after school when, as I tried to slip away unseen through the playground, a group of girls began to follow and make jeering noises at me. I could hear them giggling. When I turned, there they were, two feet away, crushed together like a bunch of asparagus (recipe to follow). Asparagus, I thought, it had been a long time since I had had asparagus. I knew just how my mother made it because I had seen her make it a thousand times. In the spring my father would drive down island and buy it off the farmstands by the bagful. Uncle Jack hadn't made green vegetables since I had moved in, but I bet he would like asparagus the way my mother cooked it. One of the girls detached herself while I was thinking about this and said, "We were just wondering, Primrose, why aren't you wearing black? Miss Honeycut told the whole class we had to be nice to you because you are bereaved."

"What do you mean?" I asked.

"Miss Honeycut sent you to the library that day so she could tell us you were in mourning. But you don't seem to be mourning."

"We think it's time you faced the fact that your parents are dead."

Another one of the girls giggled. I turned my back and started walking away faster but they kept following me.

"We just want you to know that we're here for you when you begin the mourning process," said another, hot on my heels.

"Miss Honeycut said it would happen anytime now."

"She said you would have tics, moods, and poor study habits."

"My mother says how come your mother didn't stay at home with you instead of going into that storm?"

I began to run. I could hear them running behind me. Then one girl called out, "Yeah, and your uncle's a *developer!*"

A developer, I thought to myself, as I headed onto Main Street. I didn't know what it was but it didn't sound like a good thing. I cut across a parking lot and was running down the alley between The Girl on the Red Swing and the drugstore when a hand reached out and I was pulled into a warm kitchen and safety. I stood panting and stared at my savior, Kate Bowzer, who sucked on a cigarette and looked down at me through narrowed eyes.

Miss Bowzer owned and operated the restaurant. She dragged a stool up to the stove for me, continued smoking and making waffles, and listened to my tale of woe. She made about a million waffles while I sat there. She had to make about a million every day because at The Girl on the Red Swing they served everything on a waffle. Not just the kind of food that *went* with waffles—not just ham and eggs on a waffle or strawberries on a waffle. No, at The Girl on the Red Swing if you ordered a steak it came on a waffle, if you ordered fish and chips it came on a waffle, if you ordered waffles they came on a waffle. Miss Bowzer said it gave the restaurant class. Also, she liked to give the customer a little something extra. She tossed me a couple of waffles and a glass of iced tea.

I said I had the feeling that no one was going to forgive me for not falling apart at my parents' disappearance.

"Kid, I'll tell you what no one in this town can forgive and that's that your mother loved your father enough to follow him out into that storm. Now, that's true love and it's rare as rare can be. Most of the kids in this town don't have two parents. Look around. They got one dead one and one alive one. Or they got two divorced ones who don't talk to each other. Or they've got a mom and a bird-of-the-night dad who sang one sweet song and never appeared again. And of those who have two parents how many of those wives would put on rain gear and follow their husbands out into the dark chaos of the storm, forsaking all else? It makes me weepy." She put down her cigarette, which had about a four-inch piece of ash dangling at the end of it, wiped a tear out of her eye, swore for emphasis, and took the waffles out of the waffle maker.

"I can see, then, that I am in for a rough ride," I said, munching my waffles.

"Oooo, yes," agreed Miss Bowzer, stirring the waffle batter.

"One of the girl's mothers said that my mother should have stayed at home with me."

I saw Miss Bowzer look irritated plenty of times in the years to come but I never saw her look so angry as she did right then. She dropped her spatula and said, "Why don't you get that uncle of yours—what's his name?"

"Jack."

"Yeah, Jack. I've seen him around town. He's pretty sizable. Why don't you take him over to the schoolyard and have him kick the crap out of those little stinkers."

Such a thought tickled me though I realized it was completely impracticable. The last thing I wanted to do these days was make any more waves. And at heart I was a pacifist. Well, not at heart. My mother says no one is a pacifist at heart. At heart, we're all violent raging wolves, but in our actions we can be pacifists. My mom and dad and I discussed this once when we were all sitting around the hearth. They had gone on a vacation without me for a whole week and when they got back we decided to have concentrated family time, so we made fires in the fireplace and sat around them together after dinner. At first we were just happy to be together, but our lively discussions became less lively and gathering at the hearth began to seem like a chore and finally, though no one would admit it, it became boring. Being together, like being able to see certain stars only with your peripheral vision, isn't something you can create. It's just something that happens to you.

Miss Bowzer started to get busy chopping things. I sat quietly finishing my iced tea and writing down the asparagus recipe in my mother's memo pad. I decided to use the pad to collect any recipes of my mother's I remembered or any new ones I came across that she might like. Then I put it back in my pocket, thanked Miss Bowzer for the waffles, and, sticking my head out the door to make sure the coast was still clear, headed home.

The Best Way to Make Asparagus

Snap off the ends of your asparagus. They will break off at the woodeny parts, leaving you with the tender edible stalks. Put them in a pan of water to soak. Dump the dirty water and put the asparagus in a pan of ice water with a whole tray of cubes floating in it. While they are getting cold, heat a big pan of water to boiling. Put the asparagus in the boiling water. It will stop boiling for a minute when the cold asparagus shocks it. Leave the asparagus in until the water begins boiling again. Then remove it immediately and dunk the asparagus into the ice water again. It will be cooked perfectly and you can eat it with your fingers because, as my mother always says, even kings and queens do.

The Dead Whalers

When I reached the steps in front of Uncle Jack's house, a bright new Chevy pulled up and Miss Honeycut got out. She took short mincing steps up the walkway to where I was scuttling up the front stairs to get inside and hide but wasn't fast enough.

"Is your uncle home, Primrose?" she asked.

I shook my head. Uncle Jack rarely appeared before six. Miss Honeycut shoved a plate under my nose. "I baked him these."

On the plate there were a dozen cookies (recipe to follow). It was hard to imagine her reptilian hands in the flour sack.

"For heaven's sake, Primrose," said Miss Honeycut, staring down at me. I must have looked stunned. "They're lemon sugar cookies. The kind I make for Aunt Tilly when I go back to England to visit her. She is dying of cancer. In fact, I must get back rather soon and tend to her, and I should like to see a friend in Denver who is also, I fear, dying. It's been rather a long time since I've seen either of them and one wants to see one's friends before they die, and Aunt Tilly likes it if I come and bake for her. I often make her these lemon sugar cookies since they're very like ones my uncle ate when he had tea with the Queen at one of her garden parties, which, as you know, they have at Buckingham Palace every year for quite a lot of people."

Miss Honeycut kept me on the steps for ten minutes telling me a long anecdote about the Buckingham Palace tea and giving me her aunt Tilly's favorite lemon sugar cookie recipe, her uncle Albert's favorite lemon sugar cookie recipe, her favorite lemon sugar cookie recipe, and an odd recipe for chocolate mousse. I was interested, but Miss Honeycut talked so quickly in such detail about so many people I didn't know that it got confusing and my mind wandered.

Suddenly Miss Honeycut barked, "I said, isn't that a splendid thing for a dying person to say?"

"Oh, yes," I said, and then to divert attention from my inattention, "what do you do at someone's dying bedside?"

"Read to them, of course," said Miss Honeycut.

I'm sure she thought Canadians and especially Canadian children were a bunch of heathens with no idea how to act at the bedside of dying people. And she might have been right because I kept thinking that if I'd been lying around for a while dying, I'd probably already done a lot of reading myself and wouldn't be so terribly grateful for someone coming in and doing more. I wondered why Miss Honeycut had so many dying friends. Whether she had so many friends that naturally some of them would be dying or if she liked terminally ill people and looked for them.

Just then Uncle Jack pulled up. He got out of his car with his big, bouncing, catlike step that I found so reassuring, especially when I was cowering between the front door and my guidance counselor, unable to say thank you, now go away. He was dressed in a suit, starched shirt, and tie. I could smell him from the top of the steps. He wore a lot of aftershave when he worked and used a lot of breath freshener. It didn't make him smell good exactly, more as if he was trying hard. He bounded up to us and when Miss Honeycut, who was taking in the crisp shirt and suit in an approving way, handed him the plate of lemon cookies, he gave her a huge smile that was wall-to-wall teeth from beneath his blond mustache. The smile was both a warm and gracious welcome and a polite dismissal. Miss Honeycut launched into her tea at Buckingham Palace anecdote and the grin never left Uncle Jack's face for one moment. When she finished there was silence for thirty seconds or so, then Miss Honeycut snapped it off crisply by saying through her teeth, "I hope that everything is running smoothly since the adjustment."

"The adjustment?" repeated Uncle Jack. Big smile even as he walked purposefully with her to her car. Huge smile as he opened the door for her. Bigger one as she got in.

"I mean since Primrose moved in with you. I'm her guidance counselor, you know," said Miss Honeycut, looking pinkly uncomfortable. She had a peculiar skin condition that would erupt whenever she was ill at ease. I was always surprised to see that Miss Honeycut could be uncomfortable, when it was clear she thought she was so much better than us.

"Oh, I know! I know!" said Uncle Jack. "Things are going just great. Nice of you to stop by. Always happy to hear from you. Bye-bye now." He guided me, who was huddling by him, back up the steps and turned to wave to Miss Honeycut from the top. "Thank you for the cookies!" he called. Another big smile, all teeth. Hearty wave and then we were in the house.

It was safe in the house with Uncle Jack. He was so vibrant that it was like standing next to a fire. All through dinner I gazed at the red veins in his nose. I tried not to stare but they kept popping in and out.

"Someone called you a developer today," I said finally.

Uncle Jack looked up from his dinner. He had made

four turkey TV dinners; one for me and three for himself. "That's what I am."

"Well, they didn't say it in a very nice way," I said.

"That's because not everyone wants to see Coal Harbour developed," said Uncle Jack. "But look at it this way, Primrose, what have you got here in Coal Harbour? Now that the navy's gone, you have fishing and whaling. There aren't enough fishermen to support a whole town and there won't be whaling much longer even if the folks here want to turn a blind eye to that. Already there's legislation to try to stop it because whales are becoming endangered. All these people in town who are tied to whaling are going to be out of work and the support services, the people who earn their living by providing things to everyone in the whaling industry, stores and dentists and teachers and such, will lose business too because nobody will have any money to buy anything and the whalers will have to pack up and go elsewhere. Without them there isn't enough here to keep the town alive."

I thought of all those people leaving and going elsewhere. Maybe going to the exotic places where Miss Honeycut went. Maybe having exciting, important things happen to them that wouldn't happen to them in such an out-of-the-way place as Coal Harbour.

Uncle Jack went on, "They're going to have to replace whaling with something else and that's what I'm going to do. I'm bringing in tourism. I'm doing them a big favor. They're just too pigheaded to admit it. Coal Harbour is a fantastic place."

"It is?" I asked. I had never heard anyone say that about Coal Harbour before.

"Sure. It's got mountains, it's got ocean. And when we're done developing it, it will have a great waterfront area. We'll buy up the downtown and replace those tatty stores and that god-awful restaurant with places that cater to tourists, and the money will roll in."

"I like The Girl on the Red Swing," I said. "But I wouldn't go to Coal Harbour if I were a tourist. I'd go to England or Paris or something."

"That's because you're *from* Coal Harbour, Primrose. If you were from England or Paris, you'd probably think Coal Harbour was pretty exotic."

"Oh," I said. I had never thought of it that way. Uncle Jack always looked completely calm and unflappable but his eyes were fizzing like he was a Coke can someone had shaken up.

Uncle Jack spent the next hour telling me stories about how before he went into the navy, he did some developing in the Coast Mountains.

"I found a small town in the Coast Mountains, close enough to Vancouver to be a vacation destination. That's what I figured was going to happen, all these small towns were going to become summer places for Vancouverites as the city grew. There was a building going cheap in the middle of town and I had just enough money for the down payment. My idea, as I explained to the businessmen who were ready to laugh me out of town, was to sell it to some big company. 'You aren't ever going to get anyone to buy that heap,' they said, 'and especially not some big company.' I was lunching every day at the Cattle Club where all the local bigwigs ate, even though I couldn't afford it, and they laughed at me for that too. 'Boy,' they said, 'you aren't ever going to do this deal. You better go back to where you came from and take up fishing or something else you know how to do.' "

"How did you know someone would want to buy it?" I asked.

"I *didn't* know. That's what made it so interesting! I was pumped. I was going crazy, putting out feelers here, putting out feelers there. The mortgage payments were horrific. I'd wake in the middle of the night, drenched in sweat, my heart pounding, covered in hives from nervousness."

"That sounds awful," I said.

"That was the fun part," said Uncle Jack, his eyes sparkling. "I'd sleep three hours a night and leap out of bed and back into action. Well, one day, just as I'm on the brink of foreclosure—my guts are churning, I'm juggling

26

all my other deals to see if I can get the next payment together—two men came to see me. They had an offer for
me, they said, but they couldn't disclose who they repre-
sented."

"I didn't know you could do that," I said.

"Of course you can!" shouted Uncle Jack but I knew he
wasn't shouting at me, he was just back there reliving it
all. "I knew if they wouldn't say who they were represent-
ing, I had a big fish on my line. The question was, which
fish? Which fish? I could barely stand the excitement but I
had to appear cool."

"So what did you do?" I asked.

"I jacked up my price. I jacked it up so high even I suspected I was a crazy person. I'm going to end up losing this
deal, I thought. Sure enough, they went away and I didn't
hear from them."

"Oh, no!"

"For a week. When they finally called, I wondered if I
would have to back down some to hook them. They
started off by saying that the powers that be had looked at
it and might be interested."

"So did you back down?"

"No, I said to myself, I may never be this close again.
But if I'm going to do this deal I'm going to do it my way.
I'm going to take it as far as I think I can. So I gambled
everything and said I was jacking my price up even further

for making me wait. And that very day I sold that building to McDonald's. I was only twenty-six and I had made my fortune."

"Wow," I said but I couldn't keep my eyes from wandering around that tiny base house with its junk-store furniture. Uncle Jack, who was sitting back with his legs stretched out in front of him, his hands clasped behind his head, and a dreamy smile on his face, must have noticed because he said, "Of course, the next year I lost it all again in townhouses in Vanier, Alberta. I'd been right about that little town in the Coast Mountains. Big ski resort now. But I was sure wrong about Vanier."

"You lost *all* of it?" I said.

"And then some."

"How horrible!" I said. "Your fortune had been made."

"It was only money, Primrose," he said, still glowing. "Well, I gotta go try to sell the cinnamon house." He stretched and put on his jacket.

Before that evening I'd thought business the dullest thing you could go into and the only people who went into it did so because they were so dull and unimaginative themselves. I never thought it was something that could make someone's eyes sparkle.

"What's the cinnamon house?" I asked, following Uncle Jack to the door and wishing he wouldn't go. I didn't like being alone in this new house.

"I'm running late. I'll tell you another time. Don't forget to lock up." He bounded down the steps swinging his briefcase.

I did the dishes and then went into my bedroom to do my homework. There wasn't much to military housing. Uncle Jack's had a small living room and kitchen, a bedroom, which was his, and an even tinier room in which he had put a cot and dresser for me. I got into bed and started reading but I kept hearing noises coming from the gym— swish swish swish, thuk, swish swish swish, thuk. The door from the kitchen that connected to the gym didn't have a lock. The more I thought about it, the more I thought that those noises could only be one thing—the ghosts of dead whalers playing hockey. I pulled the covers to my chin and shivered.

Finally, I got up and pushed the dresser in front of my bedroom door in case they were the kind of ghosts who used doorknobs. I did my homework and then lay awake listening to the spirits. They disappeared when Uncle Jack came back. I heard him go into the gym. He liked to do his workout and shoot baskets at the end of the day. It was hard to sleep with the echo of the dribble dribble dribble slam dunk. As I lay sleeplessly, I thought of my parents sitting on some island. I hoped they weren't too cold. I hoped they were getting enough to eat.

Aunt Tilly's Lemon Sugar Cookies

Mix together a cup of sugar and 2 sticks of butter and some salt. I don't remember how much Miss Honeycut said, so go with a pinch. Put in some grated lemon zest. Add 2 eggs and 2 teaspoons of vanilla. Beat it all together and add 2½ cups of flour. Roll it out and cut with a drinking glass into rounds and bake at 350 degrees. She didn't say how long but probably until slightly brown. That will usually do it.

I Am Almost Incarcerated

At the end of September the rains began. There were fewer and fewer days when I could go to sit on a dock to wait for my parents without getting drenched. I didn't like being at Uncle Jack's with the dead whalers, and the playground became less safe as my classmates lost patience with me completely. They seemed to think that as time went on I would admit my parents weren't coming back, but time had nothing to do with it. I didn't know what they would dare do to me beyond teasing, but I did not want to find out.

One rainy day after school, panicked by no good choices, I saw the girl who told me my mother should have stayed with me approaching. I ran pell-mell into town, where it occurred to me that I would be safe in stores. I flew into the grocery store and tried to look like an earnest shopper. Up one aisle and down another I loitered, examining the labels on the canned vegetables. I checked all the pull dates in Mr. Hardy's dairy case.

I hoped Mr. Hardy would be grateful to be told the pull dates on all his cottage cheese had expired, but he wasn't. He wished me good day, so I crossed the road and nipped into Cantina's Drugstore.

The Cantinas had a bell attached to the door that dingled when anyone went in or out. They kept a big black Labrador named Dante tied to the counter by the front door. I always gave him a pat whenever I came in. It wasn't much of a life lying there all day. I smiled at Mrs. Cantina, who was sitting at the cash register reading a magazine and eating a caramel apple (recipe to follow). Mrs. Cantina glanced up at me as if she was thinking, that's life for you, you start to eat an apple and some ugly juicy green worm sticks its head out. I swallowed my smile and went over to the magazine rack and picked up a magazine.

"Buy 'em or put 'em down," barked Mrs. Cantina, so I put it down and examined the odd sand toys that nobody ever bought.

"Can I help you?" snarled Mr. Cantina from behind the prescription counter. He looked as if he was about to say more but the bell over the door dingled and a bunch of people came in at once, which occupied both Cantinas. I took that opportunity to hide in the aisle that held

Band-Aids and hot water bottles. The bell over the door kept dingling, so I felt safe for a while and was fingering a hot water bottle when Mr. Cantina came marching down the aisle snapping, "Do you want to buy a hot water bottle or don'tcha?" and snatched it out of my hands.

I started to say, "No, I was just looking," when Mrs. Cantina squealed, "Jesus, Mary, and Maude, someone's cut Dante's leash again!"

Apparently someone had been coming in regularly, cutting Dante's leash, and letting him out of the store and the Cantinas were just mad to find the perpetrator. I stood watching Mrs. Cantina, who was running up and down the aisle making such a huge fuss that it was mesmerizing. Mr. Cantina ran to the front of the store, opened the door to call the dog, grabbed the cut leash, and swore. Mrs. Cantina stopped making gibberish noises and got on the phone to the sheriff, ordering him to come immediately and arrest someone. That's when Mr. Cantina, very stealthily, crept up behind me, grabbed my collar, and roared, "YOU!" in my ear.

No one had ever grabbed me by the collar much less roared "YOU" in my ear before. It discombobulated me totally.

"Did you cut Dante's leash? Did you? Did you? Did you?" he demanded, shaking me.

Another person, guilty or not, would have sensibly

cried "No" at that point but I was still floating these days and my mind went off on a tangent thinking it was unreasonable and silly for Mr. Cantina to keep repeating "Did you?" that way. Did he expect me to answer "No, no, no, yes"? I barely noticed the strangled gakking noises I was making as I drifted along on these thoughts when Sheriff Peters, whose office was only two doors down, strolled in.

"Hello, folks," he said.

I tried to point to myself to indicate that I was not the guilty party, but I was pretty close to fainting, so it probably came off as just a nervous tic.

"Better hand her over to me," said the sheriff. Mr. Cantina dropped me and Sheriff Peters led me to the door.

"And don't come back!" yelled Mrs. Cantina.

"Don't NEVER come back!" yelled Mr. Cantina. "She was fingering the hot water bottles!"

"I was only looking!" I protested.

The bell dingled as Sheriff Peters and I left. We walked slowly toward his office.

"I was just going to go look for you actually," said the sheriff.

"I didn't cut that leash!" I said.

"Oh, that," said the sheriff absently, which didn't seem

to me to be a very professional response from a law and order man.

We walked silently the rest of the way to the jail. My mouth was beginning to go dry at the thought of it. Then suddenly it occurred to me that a jail cell was a safe place to be. A quiet nest where people would leave me alone. And I liked Sheriff Peters. But it would be a terrible thing for Uncle Jack and even worse for my parents when they returned.

We entered the sheriff's office. Beyond his desk were two cells, clean but spare. I thought I might have trouble entertaining myself there. He went behind his desk, sighed, and said, "I've got something to show you."

He pulled out a yellow macintosh and, with a face full of pity, handed it to me. I knew it was my mother's even before I saw the inside where her name was written in big felt-pen letters to distinguish it from mine or my dad's. I looked at her felt-pen name blankly.

"Fisherman found this on one of the Queen Charlotte Islands caught on a rock. He got off his boat, Primrose, and *walked* the whole island but she wasn't there." He stopped and let this sink in.

But it didn't matter. Because all it proved was that my mother was sitting out there coatless somewhere, waiting to come home to me. Even as he stared at it, the remark

"Your mother's dead" sitting unspoken, like something rotten in our path that neither one of us wanted to be the first to pick up. Even after the kind of day I had had, being taunted at school, and then threatened with incarceration. Even knowing that when I went home I would face a house full of ghosts, it didn't matter to me. Instead I felt a little stab of joy.

Well, I thought to myself as we both continued to stare at the macintosh and the feeling of joy swept through my soul like fire up a vacuum, this is certainly inappropriate.

"Haven't you ever believed in something contrary to the evidence?" I asked.

Sheriff Peters frowned. Then he said soberly, "I once believed that a man we had caught with all the evidence of murder around him was innocent. We ended up sending him away because we had to present evidence against him."

"Was he was proved innocent?" I asked.

"No, but I continue to think after all these years that he was. And I can't give you a single good reason for it."

We looked at each other knowingly, I nodded, turned around, and went home.

Caramel Apples

This is perhaps the easiest recipe of all. Buy a bag of caramels and melt them slowly in a double boiler—that is, in a saucepan that is over a saucepan of boiling water. When the caramels have melted, take apples that you have stuck Popsicle sticks through and dip them in the caramel until they are coated. Let dry on waxed paper. Do not muck around with chocolate or nuts or anything else fancy that may tempt you. It will only gum up the works. Sometimes you get tempted to make something wonderful even better but in doing so you lose what was so wonderful to begin with.

Lena's Boiled Potatoes

When I got home from the sheriff's, Uncle Jack was in the kitchen deep-frying Tater Tots and making Buffalo chicken wings. This was my favorite of his repertoire as he very well knew, which otherwise tended toward frozen potpies and TV dinners. Next to the kitchen table was a box and in the box was a puppy. Uncle Jack wiped his hands on his apron, which he wore to protect his suit, and squatted down by me.

"What's its name?" I asked, picking it up.

"I don't know. You can name her," he said, patting her behind her ears. "One of my client's dogs had a litter a few weeks ago and they've just started to let them go. I always wanted a dog."

"You always wanted a dog but you never gave any thought to what you would name it?"

"I thought 'Puppy,' " said Uncle Jack, getting up and returning to his frying.

I put the puppy back in the box. "They found Mom's jacket on an island."

"I know," said Uncle Jack, not turning around, just wiping his hands on his greasy apron and throwing chicken wings into the deep fryer.

"How do you know?" I asked, getting up.

"Sheriff got me on my pager," said Uncle Jack, and that was the last we said about that. "I have to go off to the cinnamon house again after supper."

"Oh, yeah, what is this cinnamon house thing?" I asked, getting out the knives and forks.

"Well, Miss Bailey apparently read somewhere in some how-to-sell-your-house book that if you burn cinnamon on the stove it makes the house smell warm and inviting. The problem is that she has been burning whole jars of it in the oven, so that every time you walk in the door, the smell hits you over the head and nearly knocks you unconscious."

"Why don't you just tell her to stop?" I asked, helping Uncle Jack put dinner on the table.

"I'm going to," said Uncle Jack. "As soon as I can think of a tactful way to do it. We don't want to embarrass her and have her give the listing to someone else. I'd like to sell that house soon. I need a few quick sales right now so that I can turn around and get the townhouses and condominiums going."

We sat down and gnawed on wings.

"Why don't you take me with you on your rounds after school? Maybe I will think of something," I said.

"Never mix business with pleasure, Primrose."

"Did I ever tell you about Lena and the boiled potatoes?" I asked.

"No, I don't believe you did," said Uncle Jack, leaning back in his chair and stretching contentedly. The phone rang before I had a chance to say anything more about boiled potatoes (recipe to follow), and he had to rush out to show a house, so it wasn't until later that I got a chance to make my point.

After he left I called Miss Bowzer at the restaurant. "I was just wondering," I said, "if you have any recipes for boiled potatoes."

"For *what?*" barked Miss Bowzer. I could hear the sound of pan lids hitting the floor and general pandemonium. "I'm sorry, Primrose, but we've got a full restaurant tonight for some reason and it's a madhouse in here. Doesn't your uncle have any cookbooks?"

"No, I don't think so. He's not here. He went out to show a house," I said.

There was a pause, then Miss Bowzer said, "Well, come on over. We'll make potatoes around doing other . . . for heaven's SAKE, be careful!" she shouted at someone and hung up. I put my jacket on and dashed over and we made boiled potatoes, which Miss Bowzer heaped on the orders she was sending out—a little something extra—until it was time for bed. Then Miss Bowzer had a waiter drive me home. Uncle Jack still wasn't back and the ghosts were slamming a puck around the gym at a furious rate, but I was so tired from cooking that I fell right asleep anyway.

After school the next day I ran to Miss Perfidy's to borrow a cookbook before going home. Uncle Jack had no appointments until later, so he and I took Mallomar to the beach. I had decided to name the puppy after my favorite cookie because she was round and white-and-black like a Mallomar. We watched Mallomar chase the seagulls with great hope and purpose while I told Uncle Jack about Lena and the boiled potatoes.

"Okay, this happened last year," I said. "Every year the elementary, middle, and high schools have a big fair to raise money. There're simple rides and fishponds and cakewalks and stuff. And lots of contests for quilters, and jam makers, and chutney makers. The schools send all the kids home with a list of the different kinds of contests to enter. I had brought my list home the day Mom and I were visiting our next-door neighbor, Lena. She had moved here six months earlier with her husband and two small children. She had been a lawyer until she had her second baby and decided to stay home with her kids until they were old enough to go to school.

" 'She's kind of restless,' my mother had said to me.

"Lena was always outside sweeping her walk or cleaning her windows or putting pots of geraniums around. Once she dug up her whole tulip bed and replanted them in color-coordinated rows. My mom felt sorry for her but I didn't see why. You could tell she had the perfect life. She was always telling you so.

" 'James has taught himself to read even though he is only four, and I don't know what you do to continue to intellectually stimulate a child like that,' she said to my mother and me when we came over to visit that day.

"We looked down to where James was putting a twig up his nose and playing with his Matchbox cars.

" 'And we're all so happy here in a small town. Away from the pressures of big city life. It will be good for Ryan. I'm afraid he is a handful. If this were a larger town I would consider bringing Ryan to a therapist. I don't think he is displaying age-appropriate behavior. He is always running around.'

"We watched him chase a cat up a tree. He was very agile.

" 'He's just got a lot of energy. Boys do,' said my mother.

" 'Still, I'd like to have him tested,' said Lena.

"I suggested that she could go to see Miss Honeycut but my mother said she didn't see much point in that and changed the subject. Then we went into Lena's kitchen for milk and cookies.

"Lena had sixteen kinds of cookies on her counter.

" 'What is this for—a bake sale?' asked my mother.

" 'I wanted to find a nutritious cookie that was appealing to both children and adults alike, so I tried a few kinds this morning. After dinner I will try a few more,' said Lena. 'I think that the apricot thumbnail cookies may be close but I'm not sure that they will appeal to Ryan on a long-term basis or whether, when they are older and I pack them in school lunches, they will retain their apricot filling if the lunch bags get squished about in their knapsacks.'

" 'You ought to enter these in the cookie contest at our school fair,' I said. I showed Lena the contest list and she laughed.

" 'I love this,' she said to my mother. 'Look, a boiled potato category. Entry must include a dozen boiled potatoes.'

" 'It's harder than you'd think to make a bowl of a dozen perfectly uniform boiled potatoes,' said my mom evenly.

" 'Oh, come now, how hard can it be?' asked Lena. Then her eyes kind of glazed over.

"On the way home I said to my mother that she ought to persuade Lena to enter the cookie contest because it was easier to win and she obviously knew her way around a cookie sheet. None of our business, said my mother.

"Well, it was a slippery slope from there right through to contest day. Lena became obsessed with making a dozen perfectly boiled potatoes. She practiced day and night. Empty potato bags piled up on her back porch.

" 'Have you noticed,' my father observed, looking next door and sniffing, 'that the whole block is starting to smell like potato salad? What do they do over there?'

" 'It's just Lena and her boiled potatoes,' said my mother.

"On the day of the fair, Lena came pounding on our door. Sweat was pouring down her forehead. The front of her apron was stained. She had pieces of potatoes clinging to her shoe. 'I can't find Ryan,' she said.

" 'Oh, goodness,' said my mother, throwing down the book she had been reading. 'I'll come out and help you look.'

" 'Never mind that,' Lena said. 'I've got a pot of potatoes on the stove and six perfectly boiled ones but I can't get the other six to come right and I've run out of potatoes.' And she began to cry. 'I was just on my way to the store to get some more. Can you watch James for me?' She put James down on our doorstep, sniffled, wiped her nose on the back of her sleeve, ran to her car, and drove off to the supermarket.

"My mother and I glanced at each other and then washed off James, who appeared as if he'd been eating dirt, and walked around the neighborhood until we found Ryan, who was crawling in a neighbor's garden. When Lena's husband got home from work, my mother left James and Ryan with me and went quietly over to tell him that Lena was at the school fair waiting for the potatoes to be judged, and then while the two of them looked at the kitchen, which had potato water and imperfectly boiled potatoes everywhere, she told him what had happened earlier in the day. He thanked my mother quietly, came over to our house and got the children, and the very next week, without an explanation or goodbye, the four of them moved away."

Uncle Jack and I sat on a log.

"You do see the point of the story, don't you?" I asked.

"Well . . ." drawled Uncle Jack, so I interrupted him.

"That whole sad day of the boiled potatoes could have been avoided had my mother just taken my timely advice and told Lena to enter the cookie contest instead."

Uncle Jack looked at me blankly.

"You remember my timely advice to you about taking

45

me with you to show houses? I *know* people in town and I know their ways. You're new here. I know what people are apt to do or not to do." I was lying. Mostly I kept to myself and I thought people were extremely unpredictable.

Mallomar came racing up to us, wagging her tail and smiling. It was clear that she thought she had attained, if not her goal of vivisecting the entire bird population, at least a temporarily gull-free beach. We gave her a dog biscuit and stood up to go home.

"Never mind all that," said Uncle Jack so suddenly it made me jump. "Can you make cinnamon rolls? If you can make me some cinnamon rolls, I'll take you along the next time I show the cinnamon house."

I nodded my head. How hard could it be?

Perfectly Boiled Potatoes

The most important thing about making perfectly boiled potatoes is to start with a dozen uniform red potatoes. So go to your greengrocer or wherever you get your potatoes and don't buy a bag of them, hunt through the loose, piled-up potatoes until you find a dozen that are medium-sized and all almost exactly alike. Don't get any with scabs or strange growths or that look like they have a nose. Take them home and peel them. Put enough water in a large pot to cover your potatoes. Cook for forty minutes, putting in more water if it boils out. Drain the potatoes and put them back in the pot. Put the pot back on the burner and shake it a bit so the potatoes dry over the heat. Then they are done. Now what you do with them is a matter of taste. Some people like sour cream, some like butter and parsley. Some people like ketchup or cheese. I like mustard. But Miss Bowzer says it is nobody's business but your own what you do with your potatoes.

What Miss Bowzer Knew

"Guess what!" Uncle Jack said. He was speaking on the phone to Miss Bailey. He winked and smiled down at me. "You don't have to heat cinnamon in the oven anymore! My niece, the one, many say, so tragically orphaned by that storm"—he winked at me again and I rolled my eyes—"likes to bake cinnamon rolls and I thought, hey, why not bake them while we show Miss Bailey's house? That's right, Miss Bailey, you won't need to bother with the cinnamon anymore. Baking is a homey smell, you bet. Absolutely you should research these things before you try to sell your house. And listen, Miss Bailey, afterward, I'm going to leave the rolls for you. You're quite welcome. I'll call you when I have someone to look at the house." He hung up beaming.

"Well," I said, "I guess baking rolls will smell better than burning spices."

"We're not going to bake the rolls at her house, Primrose," said Uncle Jack. "We're going to bring them over already baked, in a pan covered in foil so she can't see that they're baked. We can leave them on top of the stove for her. She'll never even know the oven wasn't turned on."

"Won't she suspect something when she comes in and the house doesn't smell like anything?"

"With a pan of rolls sitting right there, why would she suspect anything?" said Uncle Jack. "And without that overwhelming noxious smell, I'm sure I can sell the house right away."

I tried to teach myself to make cinnamon rolls but I had never had to use yeast before. Miss Perfidy's cookbook made it sound easy, but yeast, as it turned out, was not a sure thing. In fact, I grumbled after the third day of dumping unrisen rolls (recipe with rising advice to follow) in the garbage, the only sure thing about yeast is that it doesn't do what it's supposed to.

"Don't you have anyone you could ask about this?" said Uncle Jack when he got home and saw the garbage can full of rejects. "Any friends? Any mothers of friends?"

I hadn't told Uncle Jack about Miss Bowzer teaching me to boil potatoes. I didn't know why except that he kept making such nasty remarks about her restaurant. But surely she knew about yeast. I nodded. It was time to stop saying abracadabra over the yeast bowl and time to get help.

The next day after school I knocked on the kitchen door of The Girl on the Red Swing. Miss Bowzer was smoking and making waffles. I showed her the bowl with the yeast just lying there and Miss Bowzer took a puff of her cigarette and dumped the whole thing down the sink.

"What's the matter with people these days?" she said. "Don't teach children anything. Kids can't tell time, tell left from right, make change, tie their shoes until they're teenagers practically. Your mother never teach you to cook?"

I thought about my mother. Mostly my mother sat in the kitchen with her feet propped up on the stove, listening to violin music and reading. "If I don't learn how to make cinnamon rolls, I can't go with Uncle Jack after school, and if I can't go with Uncle Jack, I'll be either arrested for shoplifting, teased because I don't believe my parents are dead, or . . ."

"I'll tell you what's dead, your yeast," said Miss Bowzer, who was good at getting to the point. "And why would anyone want to go anywhere with your uncle anyway? That's what I'd like to know."

"Uncle Jack?" I said in surprise. "What's wrong with him?"

"Plenty! Trying to pitch people out of their homes.

Making the town so expensive no one but rich people can afford to live here anymore. Wanting to buy *me* out. HUH!" She snorted and proceeded to teach me everything there was to know about yeast. I had gotten the yeast from Mr. Hardy's store and apparently he didn't bother to check the date on it.

"I didn't even know yeast had an expiration date," I said. "There's a lot of stuff you need to know to be able to cook."

"Not so much. I started when I was just slightly younger than you. Who knows, maybe you'll end up with a rival restaurant in Coal Harbour someday."

"I want to travel like Miss Honeycut first, though," I said, munching on the waffle Miss Bowzer handed me.

"What do you want to do that for?" asked Miss Bowzer, looking down at me out of squinty eyes.

"I want to go places where important things happen to you," I said.

"Why?" drawled Miss Bowzer.

"So I'll know more," I said.

"Huh," snorted Miss Bowzer. "Some people see the whole world and don't know anything. Take this uncle of yours, I bet he's been around the block a few times. Now let's see how this yeast is doing. There. Just like I said, if your water temperature's right and your yeast hasn't expired, you got nothing to worry about." I looked at the yeast, which was bubbling, while Miss Bowzer went back to airing her views on Uncle Jack. "He's already bought out the Cantinas, those spineless jellyfish—you know that?"

I didn't but I couldn't help but be happy about that.

"And some big soulless drugstore that doesn't know you and doesn't care is moving in."

I didn't see how that was going to be worse than the Cantinas, who did know you and didn't care, but I didn't say anything because I liked Miss Bowzer. And she was a lot prettier than I had first thought. At first glance she was kind of ordinary-looking—middle-aged and plump with a ring of blond, fussy hair around her head. But when I studied her up close, I saw that she had eyes like shimmering green islands.

"You ever been married?" I asked her as we labored over the dough.

"Nah," she said. She took a drag on her cigarette and blew the smoke out in a long, thin tunnel. "I don't settle. When I heard the story of your mom and dad, I said to myself, yeah, that's what I've been waiting for. I want someone who puts the whole ball of wax at risk. I want the kind of marriage where we would follow each other out into the stormy fatal sea or I'm not marrying at all."

"Wow," I said but added, "It wasn't fatal. Just stormy."

"So you say," said Miss Bowzer and took another drag on her cigarette.

My mother smoked too but I guessed by now she had quit the habit, which was, I supposed, one of the advantages of being shipwrecked. I used to poke pinholes in all her cigarettes because I had read somewhere that when you do that the smoker can't inhale. I did it because I didn't want my mother to get lung cancer and die, but when she found out it was me doing it (and I denied it as long as I could), she got very angry and wasn't touched at all by my concern. And then this storm thing came up, so I guess you can't really protect people anyhow. Or if you protect them from one thing, up and comes another.

Miss Bowzer showed me how to mix the other ingredients for the cinnamon rolls and knead the dough. As I pounded it on a floured board, turning it a quarter turn each time with the heels of my hands as instructed, I said, "What did you mean 'so you say,' when I said the shipwreck wasn't fatal?"

"I didn't mean anything. Believe what you will believe," said Miss Bowzer, peering over my shoulder, cigarette ash perilously close to the dough.

"Didn't you ever believe anything just because you knew it was true?" I asked.

"Nah," said Miss Bowzer, then she got a faraway look

in her eye. "Course there was the time I knew about the whaling ship." She stopped puffing and put her cigarette out absently. "This was back when I was a little girl. My father's whaling ship was going out to sea the next day and the night before I woke in the middle of the night covered in sweat and just scared. I was just scared for no reason at all. I sat up for an hour and shivered in my attic room in the dark, wanting to tell my mother, but I had nothing to tell! We had a house down by the docks and I could hear the waves crashing. Usually it was a sound that calmed me but that night it made me more fearful. I was pretty sure I hadn't had a nightmare. I told myself I was being ridiculous but it was as if the air was charged with waiting. Like something awful was going to happen. The next day when my father was about to leave, I awoke early and went racing downstairs and clung to his leg. I was never up that early in the morning and my father thought I had gone out of my mind. I begged him to stay home with me. I cried and cried. He kept trying to shake me off and pass me to my mother but I wouldn't let go. Then he did an odd thing. He turned to my mother and said, 'I'll stay home today, Kathleen.' Well, this was my father, who never missed a day's work since he had started on the whaling ships thirty years before, as a boy. My mother nodded and went down to the docks herself to tell the crew my father was ill. She couldn't give any other explanation. That afternoon a terrible storm arose and the whaling ship got wrecked on the west coast by Tofino. Regular graveyard for ships it is over there. Everyone went down with the ship. I'll never forget that year. Whole town in mourning. If we'd have known what was to happen we would have tried to keep the whole crew from going out that day, though doubtless no one would have believed me. The day had started clear and fine with no storm warnings. My parents never said a word to me, not one word about it. I don't know if they were scared by it or they didn't want to scare me. I felt so terrible and responsible that I blurted it all out to my aunt weeks later and she said we all live in worlds seen and unseen."

I shivered. "Suppose your father hadn't believed you?"

"Yes, suppose," said Miss Bowzer in a queer voice. Then we formed the dough into rolls and Miss Bowzer lent me a pan to take them home in. "You bake them in your own oven, that way you can eat them while they're hot. Nothing like cinnamon rolls hot out of the oven. Now, you come on over after school sometimes and I'll find other things for us to cook."

Cinnamon Rolls

This is kind of a tricky recipe. I would master caramel apples and a few other things before moving on to cinnamon rolls.

First, check your yeast and make sure the expiration date hasn't come and gone. Then pour a quarter cup of lukewarm water into a mixing bowl and put a teaspoon of sugar into it. (It is the sugar that gets the yeast all excited.) Put 2 teaspoons of yeast into the sugar water and let it fizz up for 10 minutes. If it doesn't get all excited but just lies there like mud, dump it and start over. Add 2 large beaten eggs, ½ cup of milk, ½ cup of sugar, ½ cup of flour, and 1 teaspoon vanilla. Mix this up. Then stir in 2½ cups of flour. Put the mixture on a floured surface and knead 1 stick of soft butter into the dough. This is a messy business. To knead anything turn the dough one quarter turn, fold it in half toward yourself, and kind of pound it down and forward with the heels of your hands. When it seems to be getting sticky, throw more flour on it. You keep doing this endlessly it seems, or for ten minutes—whichever comes first. Put the dough in a buttered bowl, cover it with a cloth, and let it rise until doubled in bulk. Then punch it down, roll it out, and spread the dough with melted butter. Sprinkle sugar and cinnamon all over it until it's covered and then roll it up into a tube. Slice it so that you have about 1-inch pieces. Then put these on a baking sheet and cover with a cloth and let rise again. Bake it in a 350-degree oven for about half an hour or so. Take powdered sugar and butter and milk. Miss Bowzer didn't give me very clear directions on this. She said just mix it up so that it looks like icing and I did, using about ¼ cup of butter, 2 cups of sugar, and a few drops of milk, but she said proportions here aren't crucial. Spread it in little gobs over the hot cinnamon rolls. It will melt all over them and be completely delicious.

I Lose All My Sweaters

Now that I knew how to deal with yeast, I was ready to join Uncle Jack the next time he showed the cinnamon house. He came home two nights later saying he had an appointment set up for the next day at four o'clock. I baked the rolls that night and wrapped them in foil. When I got home from school the next day, I put on my good navy dress and went over to Miss Perfidy's house to get my matching cardigan. I even used a little of Uncle Jack's breath freshener although no aftershave. I found myself slowing down as I approached Miss Perfidy's house. Uncle Jack thought it was strange that I didn't move my sweaters into his house. I said it was because the moth-balls were protecting them but really it was because I wanted to see Miss Perfidy now and then. We had a peculiar relationship. We didn't like each other much but had lived through my parents' disappearance together. It gave us a kind of melancholy bond.

I kicked brown leaves down the street. Fall was completely upon Coal Harbour, from October's orange crackling leaves to the mists and fogs that crept up from the ocean, climbing the hills and rolling in the valleys. I could see the ocean from Miss Perfidy's street, gray on top and frothing white as it tossed its way into shore. They'd better hurry and get rescued, I thought, thinking of chilly winter storms ahead.

When Miss Perfidy answered the door, I noticed that she had her dress on backwards. For the first time it occurred to me that Miss Perfidy, who must be in the neighborhood of 104 years old, might be failing. It was a disturbing thought. As long as I had known her, which was all my life, Miss Perfidy had been old. You couldn't imagine Miss Perfidy being anything but old. At this stage of the game, with so much practice being old, she wasn't going to start making mistakes because she was *getting* old. From such established oldness there was nowhere to go but dead. This gave me an uncomfortable feeling in my stomach. It also made me a little mad at Miss Perfidy. Like she wasn't trying.

"Come to get a sweater," said Miss Perfidy. It was a statement, not a question.

"I need my good sweater. I'm helping Uncle Jack later. We're making . . ." I began but Miss Perfidy was already out of the room. Going through the living room, I noticed that the doilies were missing from the chair arms. I had lived with Miss Perfidy long enough to know her cleaning routine. On Tuesdays Miss Perfidy vacuumed the furniture. She took the doilies off for this and returned them later. I followed Miss Perfidy into the kitchen.

"Are you vacuuming today?" I asked.

"What? What's that? Why, Primrose, you know very well I don't vacuum on Thursdays. This is Thursday."

"Well, your doilies are gone," I said.

"No they're not. They're just where they always are."

"On the chair arms?" I asked.

"Where else would they be?"

"I don't know," I said. I saw a funny-shaped pan on the stove and decided to change the subject. "You've got a new pan."

Miss Perfidy looked at me through narrowed eyes as I sat down across from her at the kitchen table. She was pouring herself a cup of raspberry tea and eating stale soft tea biscuits (recipe to follow). Her cookies always tasted of mothballs. She pushed the cookies in my direction and I ate one to see if the flavor had changed since I had left but it hadn't and I looked around to see where I could spit it out without her noticing.

"I got that pan from my sister, Mrs. Claire Witherspoon, who just visited. The one who lives down in Comox. I know I told you about her. She is widowed now. She and her husband ran a hardware store that she still owns but hires young people to run. She had them left over. Crepe pans. She used to run a serious hardware store with serious hardware. Then everyone got all la-di-da. Could afford to start cooking for recreation and she had to start carrying notions like crepe pans, fondue pots, cappuccino machines. The problem is, Primrose, she can't tell when a fad is over, so she always ends up with leftover junk. And so I acquired that crepe pan."

We were silent for a minute. Miss Perfidy because she was deep in thought and I because I had a mouthful of stale biscuit that I couldn't bring myself to swallow or spit out.

"At least, I think that's where I got that pan," said Miss Perfidy.

"What do you mean?" I asked finally, choking down the cookie.

"Lately, I seem to remember things incorrectly," said Miss Perfidy, rubbing her forehead.

"You mean you're losing your memory?" I asked.

"No, I've somehow acquired a whole new memory of things that never happened. The other day I called up Margaret Miller to thank her for having me to Sunday din-

ner. *Some* of my old employers invite me for Sunday dinner, Thanksgiving, Christmas, Easter." Miss Perfidy sniffed.

I felt guilty but how could my family have Miss Perfidy
over for Sunday dinner when two-thirds of them were
floating around in the Pacific? I imagined asking Miss Perfidy to share a turkey TV dinner with me and Uncle Jack.
It didn't bear thinking about.

"Margaret made a roast chicken. Little Sarah played
the piano for us afterward. Of course, she isn't really so little anymore. And I had the distinct impression that she
did not want to perform. I find that children never want
to perform when you ask them to but you can't stop them
when all you want is some peace and quiet."

"Uh-huh," I said, thinking as I had so many times that
Miss Perfidy should never have become a baby-sitter.

"Naturally I thanked her even though she had put too
much sage in the stuffing and I could have done without
the recital. That's when she told me that I had never
been there for Sunday dinner. She said that they don't
even have Sunday dinner. That Sunday dinner is usually
canned soup and grilled cheese or something. Of course,
that's true in many homes nowadays. Sunday dinner used
to be a sociable meal after church. It's too bad it didn't
happen because I remembered it clear as day and I had
quite a pleasant time."

"My," I said.

"She also said that Sarah doesn't play the piano."

We sat and thought about this.

"It could be worse," I said finally. "You could *not* remember things that *did* happen."

"My mind is as sharp as a tack. I probably have a better memory than you *that* way, anyway."

She'd almost have to, I thought, with all those extra memories floating around in there. "Well, as long as you had a good time . . ." I ventured. "I mean, if the memories are nice, you can enjoy all kinds of things that you didn't have time to do."

"I've got lots of time to do things," grumbled Miss Perfidy. "I've got nothing but time. It might be nice if I had some *control*. You don't see that this is what is so bothersome, I've got no *control*. And I won't know tomorrow if you really came over for a sweater or if it was just another memory of something that never happened. Now I must go. I have an appointment in town." She paused and looked troubled. "I think."

It must really bother her, I thought, because this was the most Miss Perfidy had ever talked to me. Miss Perfidy was getting her pocketbook off the coatrack in the hall, so I ran upstairs.

"I'll just get my sweater," I said. I went down the hall to the guest bedroom, opened the dresser, and ran back to the landing.

63

"Miss Perfidy!" I called. The front door banged as Miss Perfidy left. I went back to stare morosely at the dresser. All my sweaters were gone.

Tea Biscuits

This is really two recipes. One is the recipe for delicious tea biscuits and the other is for Miss Perfidy's tea biscuits. For delicious tea biscuits mix ⅓ cup of shortening with 1 cup of white sugar. Add 1 egg and beat until light. Then add 2 cups of cake flour, 1 teaspoon baking powder, ⅛ teaspoon baking soda, ½ teaspoon salt, and ¼ cup of sour milk. Mix it all up. Add 2 teaspoons pure vanilla extract. Drop by the spoonful on a greased cookie sheet. Bake in a 350-degree oven until done. If you prefer Miss Perfidy's tea biscuits, double the baking soda and leave out the vanilla. Then age for ten days in a drawer full of mothballs. They won't be tasty but they'll be authentic.

I Lose a Toe

I ran home, grabbed a jacket and the cinnamon rolls, and sat on the front steps waiting for Uncle Jack to pick me up and take me to the cinnamon house. When Uncle Jack pulled up, he was as calm as usual but he seemed less toothy, so in the car I asked him if anything was wrong.

"It's your friend Miss Bowzer," he said. I had told him how Miss Bowzer had helped me with the yeast because if I was going to go there to learn to cook, I didn't want to feel like I was doing it behind Uncle Jack's back. "I went to see her again about buying The Girl on the Red Swing."

"She told me she doesn't want to sell," I said.

"Everyone wants to sell," said Uncle Jack. "It's just a matter of price."

"Did she give you a price?" I asked.

"No," said Uncle Jack shortly. He seemed kind of grumpy about it. When we pulled up in front of the cin-

namon house I started to tell him how Miss Bowzer liked
The Girl on the Red Swing and was a good cook—at least
judging from her waffles—but Uncle Jack stopped listening in order to aim all his charm right at Miss Bailey, who
was standing in her driveway.

"Got the cinnamon rolls all ready for baking!" he
called cheerfully, taking long strides up to where she was
nervously digging through her purse for her car keys.
When he approached clients he took even larger strides.
It made him look bigger and more powerful. I tried taking
huge steps up to where Uncle Jack stood with Miss Bailey
but I tripped and went sprawling, skinning my knee badly.
Thank goodness Uncle Jack was carrying the pan of rolls.

"Oh, dear," said Miss Bailey. "I have some Band-Aids
inside." She looked as if she wasn't sure if she was supposed to go back in the house once she had left it. Uncle
Jack had explained to me that when you are selling a
house you don't want the buyers to even catch a glimpse
of the seller's face. You want them to look at the house as
a thing unto itself. It seemed to be full of mysterious ritual,
this business of showing a house. A car pulled up with the
family who wanted to see the house, and there we three
stood looking with dismay at my skinned knee while the
family fell out in a big pile of kids and dogs.

"I don't want dogs in the house," said Miss Bailey sotto
voce to Uncle Jack.

"Fine," said Uncle Jack. He whipped his starched handkerchief out of his top pocket and told me to press it on my knee. "I don't think she'll need a Band-Aid."

"No Band-Aid," I said, following his cue. There was a steady stream of blood dripping down the front of my leg, which made me a little sick, but had I known what was coming I would have thought it, by comparison, the merest scratch.

"I just got the carpets cleaned," said Miss Bailey, eyeing my leg warily, which sounded cruel and self-serving but I figured it just slipped out.

"I'll wait out here," I said and hobbled to lean against Uncle Jack's car. Miss Bailey smiled and got into her own car. She seemed anxious to get away and have her house shown.

Uncle Jack went long-striding up to the prospective buyers and shook their hands, greeted the children, and patted the pets. Then he told the parents that the carpets had just been cleaned with chemicals that might be toxic for animals. The parents frowned and said, oh, what about the children, and Uncle Jack said jovially, are they apt to lick the carpet? Everyone laughed and the mother said, no, in case there was any doubt on that score. Then there was more nervous laughter. The kids put the dogs back in the car and the family went bouncing into the house.

I stood outside and waited patiently. It seemed to me

that you ought to be able to see a house in ten minutes. Fifteen at most. If I was going to buy a house I would know the second I walked in the door whether or not it was the house for me, but I stood there for twenty minutes tapping my toes. I didn't even have anything to read, but I found a stack of Uncle Jack's listings on the car seat, so I looked at those. I was interested to see that the cinnamon house was the cheapest of all the houses he was selling. I knew Uncle Jack got a percentage of the final selling price, so I thought it was strange that he was concentrating so hard on the cinnamon house when it was so cheap. Finally, I took the handkerchief off my knee. It had stopped bleeding but it was pretty raw. After half an hour I considered going into the house to see what Uncle Jack was doing but decided that might annoy him, especially if he was closing a hot sale or something. To kill time, I practiced taking huge strides back and forth across the street. It did make me feel bigger and more powerful. I was in the middle of practicing a large stride in the road when I felt a trickle down my leg. My knee had started to bleed again. I bent over to put the handkerchief on it and when I started to straighten up I heard the long blast of a truck horn and saw big wheels. Then nothing.

When I woke up my first thought was that I was dead. There was a lot of bright light and an awful lot of noise. Compared to the comatose silence I had been in, it was an unbelievable racket. This must be hell, I thought, because in heaven surely they try to keep the noise down. A man leaned over me and said, "Primrose?" I blinked just like the heroines in movies. I could dimly make out some man peering at me over the shoulder of a worried-looking woman who was doing things to my wrist. I yanked my wrist away because who knows what someone's going to take it into their head to do to your wrist in hell?

"Primrose!" the voice came through a little louder.

"Huh?" I asked.

"I'm Dr. Sachs and you're in the Comox Hospital. Do you remember how you got here, Primrose?"

"My foot hurts," I said thinking that this was very vital information and maybe he ought to start there.

"What *do* you remember, Primrose?"

"Where is Uncle Jack?"

"Do you remember the accident?"

"There was a truck," I said. I was quite pleased with myself for remembering this.

"Your uncle is downstairs in the cafeteria getting some coffee," said the nurse. "You've given him quite a day. I'll go fetch him, shall I?"

It seemed strange to me that she said "shall I." You hardly ever hear anyone use "shall" anymore.

"Primrose!" said Dr. Sachs, patting my wrists. There was a lot of wrist patting going on. "Are you drifting?"

"No, I'm fine," I said and smiled weakly.

The nurse returned to say that she had sent an underling to fetch Uncle Jack. Without another word but a noble, terribly-important-things-to-do look, Dr. Sachs walked out. I thought you sure could tell who's who in a hospital by who felt they had to explain their comings and goings. I was also thinking that I was thinking a lot of things, so I guessed that, whatever else, I hadn't injured my brain.

"My foot hurts," I said to the nurse again. I thought they must surely be able to give me a Tylenol or something.

"You have injured your foot; you're very lucky," said the nurse.

"Thank you," I said because in scary situations I always think it is a good idea to be polite. Where was Uncle Jack? I wanted Uncle Jack right now and I really wanted the nurse out of the room. I was beginning to feel a little wild about it and also for some reason sick to my stomach. Just as I began to feel very very funny, Uncle Jack appeared in the doorway. He was as calm as always but he wasn't smiling. He got right to the point and explained that the truck had swerved to try to avoid my foot but my baby toe was gone.

Then there was an embarrassing period during which I threw up several times in a bedpan. After they had given me a pill, I said, "How could a truck hack off my baby toe and leave the rest of my toes intact?" This hardly seemed likely to me but, on the other hand, it wasn't the type of thing someone would make up.

"I don't know, Primrose, it just did. You also had a bad concussion and were unconscious for a while. We had you airlifted to the Comox Hospital and you'll have to stay here until you're well enough to convalesce in Coal Harbour."

In the days to follow, once I got used to being short a toe, I began to enjoy certain aspects of hospital life. Even though the truck driver who hit me had been told by witnesses that it wasn't his fault, that I had stood in the road like a stricken deer while he rounded the corner, that it was a miracle he had been able to swerve enough to avoid splatting me like a bug on his windshield, even so, he had six children of his own and he felt just awful. He kept sending over chocolates. His wife made me chocolate-covered cashews (recipe to follow) and they looked just like baby toes. I wondered if he was having his little joke with me and decided he was not and that perhaps I was simply destined to see baby toes everywhere for a while. The nurses tried to take them away from me, not because they found baby-toe-shaped chocolates macabre, but because they thought no child should eat that much candy. Uncle Jack stopped them. "Go ahead and let her eat it, she'll get sick of it eventually," he said, which oddly enough I never did. And then he went out and bought every nurse on the floor her own box of chocolates, after which they were all as gooey-eyed about him as Miss Honeycut, who turned up the next evening.

Miss Honeycut brought an envelope of get-well cards from my classmates, smiled brightly, and asked if Uncle Jack was around, but I had to disappoint her because he was back in Coal Harbour trying to sell houses.

"Oh," she said. "I expect he misses having someone to dine with in the evening. I have been thinking of having him over for dinner. Do you think he would like that?"

Before I had time to think I said, "No."

Miss Honeycut was startled but she was no more startled than I was and now I had to backtrack furiously.

"No, you see he does showings during the dinner hour," I said.

"Oh," said Miss Honeycut, looking peeved. "But that should be no problem at all. I never have caught on to your North American habit of dining at six or so. I eat at eight or often not until nine o'clock. I would think he would be pining for a little adult company. Just as I think you would have discovered by now that you would really be happier in a more traditional home environment."

"Don't worry, Miss Honeycut, both Uncle Jack and I know that my parents will be returning before long. There

are all kinds of small craft on these waters. It's just a matter of time before they are spotted on their island."

"Don't you think you ought to give that up?" asked
Miss Honeycut sharply.

"Haven't you ever just known something deep in your
heart without reason?" I asked, trying to look into her
eyes, but with Miss Honeycut you never got beyond the
first outer eye layer.

"Yes," she said, getting all crisp again. "There was the
time I was in our family's ancestral home, in Yorkshire.
There was Uncle Ned and Aunt Winifred and my great-
aunt Bertha, and tiny Penelope and my sister's second
husband's niece, Claire, and her boyfriend, Noodles . . ."

Miss Honeycut's voice droned on and on. I watched a
fly making a trip across the windowsill and became so en-
grossed that I missed most of the anecdote but I gathered
it had something to do with a séance and startling ghostly
revelations.

"And hooooow," Miss Honeycut droned on, "do you
suppose anyone could have known that if he hadn't even
known it himself? Well, as it turned out it was all an elab-
orate prank by Noodles, who had rigged a kind of table
knocker." She batted her eyes at me and I noticed the
creeping pink skin thing was beginning on her forehead.
Then she laughed uproariously. "Ah, yes, Noodles, don't
you see, always up for a joke."

"That's not what I meant exactly," I said and we sat in a state of discomfiture for several minutes. If there was anything Miss Honeycut didn't like it was silence.

"Yes, well, I do believe I will have your uncle over after all. Such care, taking a child into your house. You must be very grateful, realizing, as I'm sure you do, what an encumbrance you will be should he decide he wishes to have his own family someday. Well, we must move forward!" She stood up as if ready to do so but the only place for her to move forward was directly into the bed.

"I didn't know you had a sister," I said because her face hung over me like a full pink moon and I didn't know what to say to make her move.

"Yes, Bernice." And for one second I saw Miss Honeycut soften her plaster expression.

"Bernice?" I said.

"Yes. Well, half sister really. My father's daughter from his first marriage and twenty years older than I. But we have the Honeycut genes. We can, when we are together, communicate without even speaking. We often answer each other's unspoken questions quite specifically. It seems perfectly natural to us, although, of course, it defies rational explanation."

"THAT's the type of thing I'm talking about!" I yelled excitedly, bouncing up and down in my bed and then yelling "Ouch" as I shook the bed with all my movement.

74

"I'm sure you shouldn't be bouncing like that. And I don't know what you mean by that 'type of thing.' As far as I can see, there's no type of thing about it, it's simply something that we do," said Miss Honeycut.

Really, she was hopeless. She remained over me, eyes batting, teeth bared. I hoped she didn't drool because I was directly under her. Then, when it was clear I had nothing more to say on the subject, she turned on her heel and trotted out with a "So glad to find you in such good spirits! Do give your uncle my best."

I picked up my recipe notebook. As I read longingly of carrots in an apricot glaze, Uncle Jack poked his head through the door.

"I told Miss Honeycut you weren't coming," I said, surprised to see him.

"Yes, I know," he said, "but I had a cancellation. She caught me in the hall and told me a long story about some man named Noodles and a séance."

"Noodles fixed up some table-knocking device?"

"Something like that," said Uncle Jack, and I could tell he hadn't really paid much attention to it either.

"Did she invite you for dinner?" I asked.

"No," said Uncle Jack, looking momentarily horrified.

"She's going to. She wanted to know if you would like that," I said.

"She did, did she?" said Uncle Jack. "Miss Perfidy is on

her way up. I gave her a ride. She is staying a few days with her sister, Mrs. Witherspoon, in Comox, who is picking her up here later. She made the mistake of saying 'What was that again?' when Miss Honeycut asked her how she was and Miss Honeycut thought she hadn't heard the séance story and is telling it all over, only much louder." He smiled mischievously.

As if on cue, Miss Perfidy appeared in the doorway looking annoyed and bedraggled. Her dress was buttoned wrong and her hair stuck out at odd angles. Uncle Jack pulled a chair out for her and then said he was going to go get some coffee and offered to get something for Miss Perfidy, who wrinkled her nose and said, thank you, no.

"You've caused quite a stir," she said disapprovingly when Uncle Jack had gone. She folded her hands on her patent leather pocketbook and pursed her lips.

"Well," I said, modestly ducking my chin, "it was just an accident."

"That's not what I hear. People have been saying that you tried to do yourself in. Everyone has agreed that you have gotten stranger and stranger since your parents drowned."

"They didn't drown," I said, but arguing the point half-heartedly. "And I wasn't trying to commit suicide. Really, it never even crossed my mind."

"They say that you stood there like an empty-headed fool, daring that truck forward."

"I barely *saw* it before it hit me. I barely remember what happened, it all happened so fast."

"You were always a strange child," said Miss Perfidy, eyeing me speculatively. Then she got out a bag of mothball-smelling tea biscuits and sat there looking blankly around the room, eating them all herself.

"I can understand why I would throw myself in front of a truck if I thought my parents were dead, but I'm the only one who thinks they survived!" I pointed out.

We sat there silently for a minute while Miss Perfidy fastidiously picked crumbs off her skirt with a wet finger and ate them.

"Didn't you ever just know something, deep in your heart, for no reason?" I asked her, looking deeply into her eyes. She had very rheumy old eyes with the blue irises bleached, like a fish that's been lying dead on the beach for a while. I had to look away.

"No," she said simply.

"No?" I asked incredulously. "Never?"

"Don't be nonsensical, Primrose. I notice that you have removed all your sweaters from my guest room. Please be so good, in the future, as to inform me when I have the use of my dresser returned to me."

I sat there, mouth agape. "But I didn't take back my sweaters!"

"Every single drawer is empty. And you left all the drawers hanging open when you left. The dresser might have tipped right over. Let us be glad it did not."

"I opened all the dresser drawers looking for my sweaters," I said. "I meant to ask you where you had put them. I thought *you* had moved them." This was serious. "What do you think could have happened to them?"

"Moths," said Miss Perfidy.

I tried to imagine the army of moths necessary to do away with six heavy wool sweaters.

"Oh, Miss Perfidy," I said, "I don't think so."

"Very well, Primrose," said Miss Perfidy. "Then what do you think happened to them?"

She sat there in the ladylike way I guess she had been brought up, ankles crossed, hands folded in lap, back straight as a ramrod, making the most ridiculous suggestions. I did not know how to suggest to her what I was thinking.

"Miss Perfidy, you remember how you have been having trouble with your memory?" I said at last.

"I have told you before," said Miss Perfidy, "I have no trouble remembering what has happened. I merely have more memories than actual experiences. It isn't at all the same."

"No," I said ruminatively. "Then you don't remember anything happening to my sweaters?"

"Certainly not while I was there," she said. We sat in silence. I offered Miss Perfidy a chocolate toe and she refused. "Chocolates! At this hour! Your uncle should take them away. In my day children were allowed only milk and digestive biscuits at this hour. Where my sister and I grew up on my uncle's coffee plantation in Africa, you can bet we weren't allowed chocolates before bed."

We spent the rest of the time talking about Africa. Miss Perfidy knew quite a bit about Africa. Of course, in later years I discovered that she had never been out of Canada, but at the time it was quite engrossing.

"Is this the sister you're visiting in Comox?" I asked. "The one who gave you the crepe pan?"

"Crepes are nothing but pancakes!" said Miss Perfidy.

I didn't have an answer to this, so we sat silently. Miss Perfidy found a tea biscuit she had overlooked and finished it. Then her sister, Mrs. Witherspoon, showed up to drive her to her house. Miss Perfidy introduced her to me, and Mrs. Witherspoon, after glancing worriedly at Miss Perfidy's rat's-nest hair, took her off.

A nurse came in and asked, "What's that mothball smell?" and left.

Uncle Jack came back up and I remembered finally to ask him how come he was trying so hard to sell the cinnamon house when he had much more expensive listings.

"Because"—he grinned—"it's going to be the hardest to sell."

Later, as I lay in the dark, looking at the one star that shone through my window, with my foot throbbing, slightly sick to my stomach from too many chocolates, and worried about how I would be taunted at school if the rumor was that I was suicidal, I felt a little rush of joy. I didn't know where this joy came from. It didn't seem to need parents or ten toes or the things you think you need. It seemed to have a life of its own.

Chocolate-Covered Nuts

Miss Bowzer said that you can chocolate-coat anything. Just buy some chocolate disks and melt them in a double boiler, and then dip whatever you like in them. We tried a number of things, including, toward the end when the chocolate cooled, our fingers.

Uncle Jack's Idea

A few days later they released me to convalesce at home. After spending a few more days listening to the hockey-playing ghosts, I decided to convalesce at school.

It turned out that while I had been in the hospital Uncle Jack had ended up having dinner with Miss Honeycut, eating pear soup (recipe to follow). He said it was many things but a meal it wasn't. He had tried to interest her in any of several terrific investment opportunities that Coal Harbour now offered. She had tried to convince him that an eligible bachelor had many opportunities himself, if he was unencumbered by obligations. Uncle Jack told her that I was going to live with him no matter what. He reported this to me quite matter-of-factly when I pressured him for details. I knew he had just said this to let her down gently but it seemed to me it only gave her a greater motivation to get rid of me.

And indeed, no sooner had I returned to school than she called me into her office and said, "Primrose, I'm afraid you are becoming a danger to yourself. Children who have had emotional upsets sometimes act out and need special care. Uncles are very nice, but some children need more supervision than a single working person can provide."

I just sat quietly and tried to look normal.

"We are going to have to look into this and, in the meantime, work with you on these issues."

I didn't want to contradict her because I was afraid Miss Honeycut would think that I was acting out and I wasn't even sure what that was.

"I trust you know what issues I am referring to?"

I got the feeling that Miss Honeycut didn't even know what issues she was talking about—that she just liked using the word "issues" and would use it whenever she could slip it into the conversation. Certain people do get attached to certain words this way. I kind of liked "solarium" myself although it did not lend itself to such easy usage.

"Miss Honeycut," I said, "do you think it would help if I had a solarium?"

"A what?" Miss Honeycut flushed all red and patchy and looked at me disbelievingly.

"A solarium."

"It's funny you should mention that, Primrose. My

mother had a solarium in her house in Kent after she divorced my father but before she married the second cousin of Noodles, dear Uncle Charles, who . . ."

I studied all the certificates on the wall behind her and before I knew it she was saying "freedom of movement, don't you think?" I was saved from answering by the secretary, who came in and muttered something to Miss Honeycut, who walked to the door saying, "You can return to your room, Primrose. I've suggested to your teacher ways of dealing with these issues."

I waited apprehensively to see how my teacher planned to deal with these issues. It turned out that they just wanted me to take the class pet guinea pig, Herman, home for weekends.

"Caring for a small animal instills a sense of ourselves and others," said my teacher.

"I think it develops a sense of ourselves and others to care for small animals and build things. Like solariums," I said.

"That's the spirit," said my teacher.

I didn't see how I could help having a sense of myself and others. But, of course, none of us had any idea what we were talking about. It was just one of those situations where everyone involved feels compelled to say something, anything at all.

The teacher gave me a few instructions about caring

for Herman and tried to hand me his cage, then realized that I couldn't carry the cage and use my crutches at the same time. Two boys who were in the cloakroom grabbing their hockey sticks and backpacks offered to carry it for me.

"Why, isn't that kind of you boys," said my teacher. She handed them the cage.

It made me nervous to have them volunteer when I knew they regarded me with scorn, so I hobbled nervously behind them wondering if they were going to play a prank on me. When we reached Uncle Jack's, they put Herman on our kitchen table and I expected them to turn around and leave but they marched right into the gym, leaving me openmouthed. It wasn't pranks they were interested in, it was hockey.

As soon as the two boys had gone into the gym, more boys opened the door and came in. Most of them carried hockey sticks and pads. Occasionally one would bark, "Hi, Primrose," or "Your uncle's cool, Primrose."

"And so!" I announced indignantly that night to Uncle Jack over chicken potpies, "they marched in, without even *knocking*, and played hockey right here in your very own gym."

"I know!" said Uncle Jack, smiling, chewing, and twinkling. "Darn it, though, I wanted to tell you before they all trooped over but I guess they were anxious to get going!" he went on excitedly with food stuck in the side of his cheek like a chipmunk. He swallowed hastily. "I invited them to." He winked at me. "Great idea. Actually I got the idea from Miss Honeycut. More or less."

"Miss Honeycut?" I repeated blankly.

"That night I had dinner with her? She said she thought you were left alone too much. I'm out selling houses. You're in the house by yourself a lot."

"By myself too much?"

"She thought you might be accident-prone," said Uncle Jack, looking at his food and eating industriously. "She doesn't think you should be by yourself after school. I think she's afraid you're going to fall in the ocean, walk in front of buses, trip over curbs, who knows what, because you're not paying attention. She has all kinds of theories."

"Theories?" I said.

Uncle Jack put his knife and fork down and looked me in the eye. "You know, Primrose, there's something about sports. You can be setting fire to cats and burying them in your backyard, but as long as you're playing team sports, people think you're okay."

I thought about this. Uncle Jack always had a good game plan.

"I don't mind playing hockey, but those boys will never let me," I said.

"Ah, that's where you're wrong," said Uncle Jack, smiling, chewing, and winking again. "I told them they could come in anytime and use the gym. No sense trying to play street hockey now that the rainy season has started. We've got a gym that goes all but unused. I said that the only stipulation was that they had to find a disabled goalie. And not just disabled, one that had lost a *toe!*"

I digested this silently.

"Of course, you don't have to play, Primrose," said Uncle Jack. "But if you do, there you go, you have a game all set up. You hardly need your crutches anymore. You can balance yourself on your goalie stick."

So I waited. I sat at that Formica table all week while boys trooped in and out, waiting for them to ask me to be goalie. Nothing. I grabbed the gym door, threw it open, and whispered hoarsely, "What about the deal you made with my uncle Jack?"

There was a breathless silence when they saw me but only Mike Muskegon was near enough to hear me. He gave me a very sour look and said, "We got us a goalie."

I looked over to the net. They certainly had. His name was Spinky Caldwater and he was a Cambodian orphan. His mother was a single woman who wanted a child and flew to Cambodia to get him. Everybody felt sorry for Spinky. Not because he was a Cambodian war orphan or because his foot had been blown off by a land mine but because his mother was such a twit. She made him wear a necktie everywhere.

I decided to take Mallomar out for a run. We went down to the docks to sit and wait for my parents.

Pear Soup

Miss Bowzer invented this recipe. Neither one of us wanted to ask Miss Honeycut for one. Put 4 cups of chicken broth and 1 cup of white wine in a big pot. Peel and core 6 pears and poach them in the chicken broth and wine until soft. Puree. Add 1 cup of crumbled Stilton cheese and 1 cup of grated Gruyère cheese. Stir at low heat until the cheese is melted. Serve garnished with garlic croutons.

I Set Fire to a Guinea Pig

As I stood on the pier watching Mallomar do crazy puppy runs up and down the beach, chasing the birds with her great faith, I saw three seals swimming across the horizon. When seals swim together they go in single file, their dark bodies sewing a seam through the waves. All you can see from shore are their backs in a row, like one long humpbacked creature. The Loch Ness Monster and all those other sea monsters were probably nothing more than seals. There's nothing spectacular about it and yet it always makes me catch my breath.

One summer when our family was in our skiff going up the Johnstone Strait, we saw a pod of orcas coming. My father explained that killer whales live in little families. He, like most of the fishermen in these straits, knew most of the pods and could recognize individual whales by their unique markings. My dad had read all about these pods because they were his neighbors during the long days he spent at sea. This pod, he said, had recently had a seventy-year-old grandmother die and a new calf born. There were five of them swimming together perfectly in sync, in and out of the waves so harmoniously and peacefully, that I felt like an outsider in these familiar waters. All morning we followed the whales up the strait, lost to time. Sometimes the whales would disappear for ten minutes or so and then resurface someplace else to begin their rhythmic gliding. We'd gasp on each occasion and shout, "There they are! There they are!" as if seeing them for the first time. After a bit the whales moved in close to shore and swam for a long while along it. "They're sleeping now," said my dad. It amazed me that they could keep moving like this even when they were sound asleep. It was as if they had been wound up at the beginning of time and then let go into eternity.

I was remembering this, staring at the seals, and thinking of all things wound at the beginning of time when I became suddenly aware that I was the only person in the world at this moment watching these seals. I walked to the end of the pier to get a closer look when suddenly I heard someone shout, "For heaven's sake, Primrose, what are you doing standing out there in the rain?" I turned around and saw that Miss Honeycut had pulled into the parking lot of the Anglican church across the street and was unloading boxes from her car. A feathery rain had begun to fall while I was on the dock but I had been too distracted to mind. Then I noticed that the parking lot was strewn with boxes and little old ladies in orthopedic shoes, including Miss Perfidy, who went to the same church as Miss Honeycut. They were probably getting ready for a rummage sale. The Anglican church was always having rummage sales, but for a second I had a vision of the tide leaving the shore littered with old ladies the way it washes up kelp.

As I stood gawking, Miss Perfidy started talking in a loud voice about how I had always been a strange lone child. "Her mother was the same, she used to count telephone poles, and her mother's mother before her, she used to sit in corners weaving indigo pot holders." A little cluster of old ladies had gathered around her as she moved across the beach. She was much more interesting now that she had all these false memories.

"I was looking at the seals," I protested, pointing. Miss Honeycut and Miss Perfidy advanced on me separately and the old ladies returned to their boxes.

"It's just as I said, poor supervision," said Miss Honeycut.

"Stranger and stranger," said Miss Perfidy. "Not enough sense to come in out of the rain."

Miss Perfidy and Miss Honeycut reached me on the end of the pier. There were two lines of seals now, moving through the water in parallel rows as if they'd choreographed it. "Look!" I said, pointing again.

"Rather a good assortment of donations," said Miss Honeycut to Miss Perfidy politely.

"Haven't unpacked them yet. Never know until you unpack them. People use the opportunity to get rid of junk if you ask me," said Miss Perfidy.

Both of them had turned their backs on the seals.

"Yes, but you know what they say, one man's junk is another man's treasure. I remember a jumble sale we had once in a Yorkshire dale . . ." began Miss Honeycut.

I continued watching the seals. I wondered if Miss Honeycut ever looked out the window as she played bridge all the way across China.

"I *said*, I'm giving Miss Perfidy a lift home and I will drop you off while I'm at it," said Miss Honeycut.

"Oh, all right, thanks," I said.

I had to call Mallomar while Miss Honeycut took her boxes into the church. Then she and Miss Perfidy got in the front of the car and I got in the back with Mallomar, who lay on top of some newspapers Miss Honeycut had put down for her. She smelled like wet dogs do, which made Miss Perfidy sniff all the way to Uncle Jack's. When we got there the boys were still playing hockey and Miss Perfidy said she thought it was highly inappropriate to leave me with a house full of boys. Mallomar started barking loudly at Herman and Miss Honeycut looked a bit wild-eyed. I could tell she was getting tired of all of us. I solved the problem by saying I was taking Herman over to see Miss Bowzer. Miss Honeycut insisted on dropping us there before taking Miss Perfidy home.

As we pulled up in front of The Girl on the Red Swing, I asked Miss Perfidy whether she had found my sweaters yet. She said no, so sharply that in order to change the subject I asked if she had remembered anything yet that she had ever known, just known for no reason. She looked back at me and said, "Let me assure you, Primrose, that it may not be fashionable but I always know what I know for a reason and I always know the reason that I know what I know. And that is how I keep an orderly life."

One of the reasons that I liked Miss Bowzer is that when she opened the alley door to The Girl on the Red Swing and saw me standing with Miss Honeycut and a guinea pig, she simply raised one eyebrow, took me by the forearm, and yanked me in, cutting Miss Honeycut off mid-no-proper-supervision-explanation and saving us all a lot of nonsense.

"I'll take it from here," Miss Bowzer said to her, smiling

with her Irish eyes in a way that was probably very insincere but very effective.

Miss Bowzer eyed Herman narrowly and fed him a piece of carrot. "Isn't he cute? You have to get him out of here. Health regulations."

"Where can I put him?" I asked. I couldn't leave him in the restaurant because there were people eating in there and I didn't want to stick him in the alley where anyone could come by and swipe him.

The same thought seemed to occur to Miss Bowzer but she was very busy getting a couple of early dinner orders done, so she just gestured for me to put him on a stool, which I did. After all, what harm could he do? He was in a cage.

I watched Miss Bowzer bustle around the kitchen, not exactly poetry in motion—dropping a lot of stuff and throwing things about. There was flour and butter everywhere and yet she got those dishes cooked and out the door on their waffles before you could say Jack Robinson. She had to deliver them to the tables because she didn't have any waitresses until later at night when things got busier. Then she came in and wiped her forehead, apparently having forgotten Herman. To make sure she did, I covered his cage with an old stained apron and moved the stool closer to the oven and out of her path.

Then she told me she was going to teach me how to

make tuna noodle casserole (recipe to follow). She started gathering ingredients and turning waffle irons at the same time.

"That's just as easy as can be," I said in wonder, looking at the simple ingredients. "I'm going to make this for me and Uncle Jack."

"I wouldn't do that," said Miss Bowzer. "Isn't he the big gourmet? You know, he came in here and wanted me to change my menu. Crispy fresh wild greens in a light dressing of walnut oil and tarragon vinegar. I know his sort."

"Oh, no," I said. "We eat mostly potpies and turkey TV dinners."

"You don't say," said Miss Bowzer and I could see she was mentally filing this under general ammunition, so I decided not to say anything else about Uncle Jack. I liked both of them so much I couldn't imagine why they didn't like each other. As we stirred things into the casserole I kept sniffing and finally said, "Something smells funny. Is that the tuna?"

"Nah, tuna smells like tuna, what are you talking about?" Miss Bowzer said. She was very busy between giving me instructions and keeping her eye on the waffles.

"Well, are the waffles burning or something?" I asked.

"Hey, I haven't burned a waffle in twenty years," said Miss Bowzer and kept flipping them out and pouring fresh batter in. "Okay, chips up in the cabinet over the . . .

something does smell odd, are the burners off . . . oh MY GOD!"

I followed her eyes and we both raced across the kitchen. Herman was on fire.

Well, he didn't burn to a cinder or anything because, although one of the apron strings had caught fire and ignited the wood chips in his cage, we got him out before anything worse than a light singeing of his fur had occurred. Still, it was bad enough. I thought it best to leave then because I didn't want Miss Bowzer to get in trouble over having a guinea pig in her restaurant. I told her I would tell no one and she left everything to a waiter who had just arrived and drove us home.

Tuna Noodle Casserole

Blend 1 can of condensed cream of mushroom soup, ⅓ cup of milk, 1 can of oil-packed tuna, drained, 1 cup of cooked peas, and 4 cups of cooked noodles in a casserole dish. Top with crushed potato chips and shredded cheddar cheese. I am sure you can look at your casserole and decide how much potato chips and cheese you want on top. Maybe more. Maybe less. Bake in a 350-degree oven for half an hour or so.

This is a variation. Miss Bowzer says everyone likes a little variation now and then.

Ming Dynasty Tuna Casserole

Blend 1 can of chow mein noodles, 1 can of water chestnuts, 1 can of condensed cream of mushroom soup, 1 cup of cream, 1 cup of chopped veggies such as green pepper, little onions, celery, carrots, whatever you have around, 1 can of tuna fish, 1 cup of cashew pieces. Bake uncovered in a casserole dish for half an hour or so in a 350-degree oven.

Dinner at The Girl on the Red Swing

I spent the whole weekend trying to trim the singed part of Herman's fur so it wouldn't show, which resulted in a very peculiar haircut. Naturally my teacher noticed and was concerned and I ended up in Miss Honeycut's office in what was supposed to be the first of a series of counseling sessions.

"So, you felt the need to cut all of Herman's hair off this weekend," said Miss Honeycut. "What would you say precipitated this attack on a small helpless animal?"

"No, it wasn't like that at all. I—" I began when Miss Honeycut cut in.

"It isn't like sheepshearing, you know, where the animal needs to be sheared. In the farms our family owns around our manor house, where our tenant farmers work . . ." Miss Honeycut's voice droned on while I studied her. I thought she must be the one who was pining for company. It was too bad that she had chosen Uncle Jack to get a crush on, because there wasn't a hope that she would snare him. I thought she would be good company for someone, though. Someone who liked very long stories. She had traveled to so many places and knew so many people. And she showed very good taste in picking Uncle Jack, you had to give her that. I listened for a second, she was rambling about her boarding school days. It must be terrible being sent away to boarding school. No wonder she seemed so cold and proper. You couldn't help the way you had been brought up, I was thinking when suddenly she snapped, "I *said*, and wasn't that just the most remarkable thing, Primrose?" She looked daggers at me and I, who had been tilting my chair back on two legs for the small entertainment value it offered, fell with a startled crash to the floor with Miss Honeycut looking both dismayed and irritated. Before she could say anything she was summoned from her office to the AV room, where Spinky Caldwater had gotten his necktie stuck in the self-threading movie projector and was screaming uncontrollably. I felt badly for Spinky, whose luck was worse than my own, but his timing couldn't have been better. The closing bell rang and before Miss Honeycut had a chance to get back to her office I slipped out and hobbled home.

I sat at the kitchen table while boys filed into the

house, including Spinky, who had calmed down. He got his tie caught in something a couple of times a week and was probably used to it.

I watched the game in disgust for a while and then took Mallomar and went down to the beach to give her a run. She started out after the birds with all her characteristic vim and vigor but toward the end she would look up at the birds and kind of fade out. Puppydom was passing too quickly, I thought sadly, and before we knew it she would be one of those old dogs who just want to lie in the sun all day.

Uncle Jack and I were meeting at The Girl on the Red Swing for dinner. Uncle Jack had never eaten there and although he said that the menu did not look promising, he wished to sample the fare before resuming his campaign to move Miss Bowzer off Main Street and establish a classier restaurant. I felt funny going in through the front door. I waited for Uncle Jack in the area between the door to the street and the inside door to the restaurant. It was warm and had a gumball machine, a peanut machine, and a Smarties candy machine. I didn't think Uncle Jack would find this highbrow enough for his taste, so I tried to stand in front of them to block his view. But when he joined me I could see that he had glimpsed them, though he didn't say anything. He knew I was rooting for Miss Bowzer.

"Well, shall we?" he said. I knew he didn't plan to change his mind about The Girl on the Red Swing because he grinned at me with his megawatt smile and turned on the full force of his charm. On me! Who knew it for the sales device it was! Nevertheless, I succumbed. Such was the power of his smile.

Uncle Jack held the door open for me. I smiled back and stepped through looking up at him and not watching where I was going. I stepped right into Miss Honeycut, who was waiting in the please-wait-to-be-seated area. She was with a bunch of teachers. Just then the hostess came to seat Miss Honeycut's group. She waved her friends on ahead and said she would join them in a minute.

"Primrose!" she said briskly. She was a very brisk person, as if the three of us were constantly late for our trains and only she could get us organized and on our tracks on time. "Jack, so nice to see you. I think we should make an appointment to have a chat."

"Certainly," said Uncle Jack, smiling and looking trapped.

"We have to examine what has happened to Primrose in the little while since her parents have been . . . away," she said. I didn't know why she had decided to go all subtle suddenly. For months she had been telling me my parents were dead and drowned with no tact whatsoever.

"Where do you live, Miss Honeycut?" asked Uncle

Jack, his brow furrowing as if he had suddenly thought of something desperately important. There was a thin line of beaded sweat around the top of his forehead and I, who knew his furnace, could tell by the huffing and puffing of the veins in his nose that he was working his will against hers.

"Where do I live?" Miss Honeycut blinked and her mouth fell slightly open.

Uncle Jack tilted his head to the side and looked earnest.

"Why, why, on State Street. You've been there," said Miss Honeycut. She looked thrown off balance

"Lovely place," said Uncle Jack.

"It's adequate for my purposes. Why exactly are you asking me this?" asked Miss Honeycut, recovering her balance and getting all crisp and businesslike again.

"Adequate," repeated Uncle Jack, nodding as if whole books could be written about this word. "Not much of a view there on State."

There certainly wasn't. Coal Harbour didn't have many apartments and the few ugly apartment blocks on State were sandwiched between what used to be the naval base and the whale-processing plant.

"You know, it amazes me it has taken anyone this long to start building on the waterfront. I was just checking some townhouse units that will be ready for occupation

soon. Two stories, two bedrooms, picture windows open-
ing over the bay, all new lino, carpet, appliances."

"Yes, I remember you mentioning them when last we
spoke," said Miss Honeycut curtly.

"All new lino!" I echoed enthusiastically, wondering
what lino was.

Uncle Jack and Miss Honeycut looked down and gave
me the same identical thin smile and went back to their
conversation.

"Yes, and I remember you wanting to speak to me
about Primrose when last we spoke. Hey, did you hear
about the hockey games in our gym? All these nice young
men coming over to play hockey every day after school."

"Yes, and frankly, it surprises me to hear that Primrose
was playing hockey with that big bandage on her foot and
those crutches," said Miss Honeycut. "But even if she was,
I do not see what bearing it has on the haircut she gave
the guinea pig put in her trust."

Uncle Jack was momentarily stymied. This was the first
he had heard about Herman's haircut. "You know, I used
to give my cat a haircut when I was a kid. Kids do the
durnedest things, don't they? And, of course, she can
manage the position of goalie. She hobbles around the
house on her heel without her crutches most of the time
these days and only uses them for walking outdoors."

"Yes, but," said Miss Honeycut.

"And I wouldn't suggest you move if you have found a place that exactly suits your needs and you feel attached to it but, gosh, you ought to come up and see the sunsets over the ocean. Ever seen the sun drop into the Pacific? Now, there's a sight."

"Well, yes, now . . ."

"How nice to sit out on your own balcony every night with a margarita, watching that sun go down."

"I don't drink margaritas."

"I know you've got Primrose's best interests at heart. I'm sure we all do. Now, I've got a beaut of a townhouse going to be finished up this week. We could have the papers signed and you moved in by the end of two weeks. You can't beat that. And there's some amazing investment opportunities here in town. Within five years I expect real estate prices here will have doubled like they did in the towns farther south. I wouldn't do this for everyone, but we could talk about letting you have that townhouse *at cost*. And I'd even pick up the moving expenses."

Miss Honeycut stood there like a stone. She looked at me as if she was trying to figure out what in the world anyone saw in me. Her tongue worked around in her mouth. Uncle Jack was very still, hardly breathing, but smiling at her, willing her to take the bait. All three of us knew that if she tried to take me away from Uncle Jack she was going to miss the deal of a century.

"Well," Miss Honeycut said finally, "I must join my friends."

"What do you think that means?" I asked Uncle Jack as the hostess led us to a table.

"I think it means she plans to think about this when she gets home," said Uncle Jack.

"But what does she care, really, about getting a townhouse at cost?" I asked. "She's got lots of money and she won't even live here anymore when she inherits her millions."

"Oh, but, Primrose," said Uncle Jack, reading his menu. "The rich are notoriously cheap. That's how they became the rich. Now, what's good at this hash house?"

"Shepherd's pie?" I ventured. "She makes it with lots of gravy."

Uncle Jack was very partial to gravy but he went with the broiled swordfish, which he said was the most upscale thing on the menu.

"Aw, now you see, Primrose," he said when it was served. "It's a good piece of fish, nice flavor, done to perfection. If the woman would only get rid of the waffles!"

"That's the best part," I said, crunching away on mine. It was an interesting mix of flavors. I had ordered shepherd's pie (recipe to follow) and the gravy had seeped into the waffle. Miss Bowzer kept pitchers of maple syrup on all the tables. The gravy and the syrup had a certain savory-sweet charm. "Yum," I said.

Over dinner I told Uncle Jack about Miss Honeycut and Miss Perfidy dragging me away from the seals.

"I don't know how I'm going to take Mallomar down to the beach or sit on the dock and watch for my parents if everyone thinks I can't even take care of myself anymore," I complained.

"Sell fish," said Uncle Jack.

"Huh?" I said.

"To the mink farm. Mr. Contram pays ten cents a pound. All those hockey-playing boys do it when they need spare change. They wait for a whale to get towed in. The fish follow the whale. Why, haven't you noticed that the whole bay is teeming with them, feeding on each other and the carcass? Easiest thing in the world. I've seen them do it. You just dip in a net and scoop them up."

"But I'm not interested in fishing and selling fish."

"Sure you are," said Uncle Jack, leaning back and wiping his mouth. "Because you can go out on the dock holding your net and no one will worry that you're just mooning about. It will look like you're cheerfully and gainfully employed. It's . . . your . . . cover." He hissed the last dramatically.

Well, Uncle Jack always had a solution for everything and this one would have been just about perfect if it hadn't gone so wrong and landed me in a foster home.

Shepherd's Pie

When I asked Miss Bowzer for a recipe for shepherd's pie, she laughed hollowly. She said that shepherd's pie was designed to be a hodgepodge of things leftover. A thrifty recipe. However, when pressed, this is what she suggested: Brown a pound of ground beef, with a cup of chopped onion. Add whatever you have around, some frozen mixed vegetables, some peas, some corn, whatever. Also add 2 tablespoons of flour and some water and some Lipton onion soup mix so that you have gravy. Then season with whatever you like, some teriyaki sauce, some soy sauce, some steak spice, garlic, thyme, dill, just toss it all in. Take about 3 cups or so of mashed potatoes (if you don't have those around you'll have to make them), add a couple of eggs, about ½ cup of flour, a teaspoon baking powder, salt and pepper, and mix it all up, and then spread it on top of the meat mixture, right on the skillet if you have an ovenproof skillet. Bake in a 350-degree oven until the top puffs up, browns, and cooks. Don't get confused and put ice cream on it. That was her little joke.

I Lose Another Digit

Evie and Bert were real nice and I even liked their little cockapoo, Quincehead. They lived in Nanaimo and hadn't been fortunate enough to have children. They had been too old to adopt and hadn't even had much luck getting their hands on a foster child until me. Although I was happy to provide them with some measure of happiness, it wasn't home and after a while I was restless beyond belief. They never asked me to confide in them but after two weeks I knew what a strain this must have been for Evie, so one day I sat them down and laid out the whole story, most of which you already know except for the part that finally landed me with Evie and Bert.

"So," I finished up after an hour, as, eyes glued to me, they rocked in their rocking chairs and fed Quincehead niblets of chopped-up steak absentmindedly from a bowl in Evie's lap, "Uncle Jack got me a net and I would go down to the docks to wait and watch for a whale to bring my parents in. Everyone left me alone because it looked like I was fishing and they were used to kids down there trying to scoop up fish for the mink farm. Occasionally, of course, I would have to catch a fish."

"Occasionally she would have to catch a fish to make her more *believable*," interrupted Evie, turning to Bert. I was used to this by then. Evie liked to interpret things for Bert, which wasn't because Bert wasn't smart. It was just her way. That and fussing around him, running in little circles like Quincehead when he wanted out.

"Right," I said. "More believable. But anyhow, one day I was lying there facedown on the dock."

"You must have been on your stomach!" said Evie, her face crinkling in excitement. I couldn't figure out how old Evie was. She had deep wrinkles, crevices really, and flame-red dyed hair. Both she and Bert were short and round. I was almost as tall as they were, especially when Evie took off the high heels she wore all the time, even with pants. She had constantly surprised eyes, which at first made you feel flattered that you were saying so many amazing things until you realized you weren't. Because of their rounded middles and short bodies, Evie and Bert looked like a couple of kindly old hard-boiled eggs.

"I was," I continued. "I was on my stomach and I was watching the waves come slopping by, wave after wave after wave after wave after wave. I had been lying there for a long time."

"Now how long would you say that was, Primrose?" asked Bert, who always liked to get his facts straight.

"She don't know. She was hypnotized by those waves, weren't you, Primrose?"

"Well, yes, I was!" I said.

"Uh-huh. I could tell. She was hypnotized by those waves, Bert."

"Ohhh," said Bert, nodding affably.

"So she had no track of time," said Evie.

"No, I didn't," I said. "And then this strange thing happened. I began to feel like I was a wave too. And a fish." I looked up to see how they were taking this.

"Just like Evie's BEE STING!" cried Bert.

"It is! Forevermore, it is! It's my bee sting all over again, ain't it, Bert?" said Evie, popping up onto her short legs in excitement.

"It sure is, honeybun," said Bert. "You see, I was sittin' here in this very chair one day and Evie was out sunning on the lawn when suddenly she goes crashing through the door and passes out on that very floor."

"Right here," said Evie, walking over and marking the spot with the toe of her high heel.

"I was stone-cold scared. Never been so scared in all my livelong days. I called nine-one-one and they sent an ambulance quick but I thought I was losing her she was so cold and her heart was so slow."

"You were losing me, Bert," said Evie. "I was nearly done away."

"What happened?" I asked.

"I had been stung by a bee and as I came through the door I just had time to yell, 'Bert, I was stung!' before going into anaphylactic shock. Of course, we didn't know what it was called until later when I woke up with all these medicos hanging on my every word. But Bert had the good sense to tell the ambulance men that that's what I said and they said my pressure was going down and they was losing me."

"I cried like a baby," said Bert.

"Anyway, this isn't important to you, the part that reminds me is that I told Bert later that as I was sinking into that big sleep I had this sudden feeling that, you know, we think we're all separate, but you know what? We're not! We're all connected; the birds and leaves and wind and everything. We're all one thing. Also it was very relaxing. You remember me saying that, Bert?"

"I remember," said Bert. "Evie's a very relaxed person, anyway."

"Not like that. I never had relaxation that good. That was *deep* relaxation, Bert. I was floating. I was a bird. I was the sky . . ." Evie's voice drifted off into pleasant reveries.

"Exactly!" I said. "So I was kind of absorbed and leaned down to look deeper into the water when a big wave washed over me, knocking me off balance. I fell off the dock. I had the net in one hand and it got wrapped around my wrist. My fingers twisted in the netting and the whole thing hooked over the dock post, attaching me by one arm to the dock. The waves swept me up and down and in and over until I couldn't tell where there was water and where there was air and I thought I was going to drown, pulled to pieces by the sea."

"And then she'd never find out what happened to her sweaters, Bert," Evie said, poking Bert, who sometimes drifted off in his rocker.

"A fisherman onshore saw me and yelled and a bunch of men came running and untangled me and got me back onto the dock. My hand was all mangled and I remember thinking, 'It's another little trip to the hospital for me.' That's where I lost the tip of this ring finger," I said, holding up my left hand with the missing fingertip. "While I was in the hospital, Miss Honeycut gave Child Protective Services a whole file about me, saying she didn't think I was being well supervised, I had lost a toe and part of a finger in Uncle Jack's care, and they sent me down here while they reviewed things."

"Well, I hope your uncle Jack didn't give Miss Honeycut a good price on that townhouse," said Evie.

"She had already signed the papers to buy it at cost the day after we met her in the restaurant, so he couldn't take it back and he was mad as a hornet. He accused her of getting rid of me for her own purposes and she said, 'And what would those be, Mr. Dion?' He couldn't very well say, to snare *him*, without sounding like a conceited fool, so he just stormed around and spluttered. I guess she's kind of given up on him, though, because she used to call him Jack. Anyhow, she claimed to have nothing but my welfare at heart and maybe she does because, after all, she is bred to the nobility, so she has to do the right thing no matter what. I told Uncle Jack that I thought since she was raised in boarding schools she probably didn't think anything of sending a child away from her home if she thought it was in the best interest of the child. Uncle Jack said she was a cold, cold fish but I get glimpses of a good heart sometimes, like when she talks about her sister or all those deathbed visits she makes."

"Well, I think she's just a big cheater," said Evie.

"Well, anyhow, you can see that none of it was Uncle Jack's fault."

"Well, we can see that," said Bert.

"Sure, we can see that," said Evie.

"So we hope you get to go back to Coal Harbour even though we would miss you," said Bert.

"You've been like a daughter to us," said Evie, holding

up the sweater she was knitting for me against my back to see if it would fit.

"Better than a daughter if you ask me," said Bert.

"Sure, because what Bert means is that we'd already know our flesh-and-blood daughter's stories but you got stories we never heard."

"You're more entertaining than a flesh-and-blood daughter," said Bert.

"Which we never could have," said Evie.

"Well, it's too bad about that," I said.

"You miss your home, don'tcha?" asked Evie.

I started to cry. I knew my parents were coming home someday but in the meantime I did miss my home. Not my home with Uncle Jack, nice as he was, but my own home with the sound of my mother's footsteps in the morning as I lay still in bed and the sound of my father's coming up the front walk at night. Evie cried too, saying she missed the child that had never been born. I had been eating butterscotch chow mein noodle cookies (recipe to follow) steadily since getting home from school and suddenly regretted the last eight or nine.

"But I'm not miserable all the time," I snuffled sometime later when I could breathe. We had gone through most of a box of Kleenex. "Sometimes I get these bursts of joy."

"Me too!" sobbed Evie. "You can be sunk low as a

skunk and still have a joy in your heart. Joy just lives like one of those spinning things, what're they called, Bert?"

"Gyroscope?" said Bert.

"He always knows what I mean. Gyroscope in your chest. It don't seem to have any connection to circumstance, good or bad. Have a mint." She was always passing out mints.

"Ain't it the truth?" said Bert, who had been very helpful holding the tissue box.

"I know!" said Evie, hopping up and down on her high heels. "Let's go to that restaurant you like so much. What's it called?"

"The Girl on the Red Swing?" I said.

"Sure, why not? What do you say, Bert?" she asked.

"Chinese is our favorite," said Bert.

"We've been to every Chinese restaurant in Europe!" interrupted Evie excitedly. "The Paris Chinese restaurants, they got nothing on the ones in Italy. But you know where you find the very best?"

"China?" I ventured.

"China isn't in Europe, honey. London. Gosh, they got great Chinese restaurants in London, don't they, Bert?" said Evie.

"They probably *do* have the best Chinese restaurants in China," said Bert.

"But they probably don't *call* them Chinese there. No one in China says let's go out for Chinese food," said Evie.

"They just say let's go out or let's go eat," said Bert.

"Well, The Girl on the Red Swing isn't Chinese," I said doubtfully.

"Don't you worry about that," said Eve. "We'll take Quincehead."

"I don't know if Miss Bowzer allows dogs in the restaurant," I said.

"Oh, Quincehead's real nice and quiet. I'll just keep him in my lap and feed him scraps under my napkin. We did that on our trip down to Arizona, didn't we, Bert?"

"Uh-huh," said Bert.

"You really travel a lot," I said.

"We like it," said Evie.

"Keeps us young," said Bert.

"And she's gotta go home, Bert," said Evie. "If only just to see the place."

"Oh, I know," said Bert.

"She don't even know what happened to her sweaters!" said Evie. I followed Evie up to her room and watched as she began packing an overnight case. "We'll leave in the morning. We'll stay in a motel. We won't put no one out that way. You'll probably have to stay with us, honey, seeing as how you're a ward of the province these days. But we'll take you to see your uncle Jack and everything will be fine."

And, of course, eventually she was right.

Butterscotch Chow Mein Noodle Cookies

Here you have it: something that is exactly what it says it is. Take a 12-ounce package of butterscotch chips, a can of chow mein noodles, and 2 cups of salted peanuts. Melt butterscotch chips in the microwave or in a double boiler. Remove from heat and immediately stir in the noodles and nuts. Drop by the spoonful on waxed paper and let cool.

Fire!

You're probably wondering what was going on with Uncle Jack through all this and thinking that in regards to nieces it was just easy come, easy go to him, but not at all. He was fighting those Child Protective Services folks tooth and claw for me, and calling constantly with progress reports. When we got up to Coal Harbour and checked into the motel, he was excited to give us the latest, and raced to meet us for dinner at The Girl on the Red Swing.

Evie and Bert really liked The Girl on the Red Swing.

"Look, Bert, that's her," said Evie, pointing to the mannequin hanging from the trapeze in the middle of the restaurant. "That's the *girl* on the *red swing*."

"That's probably why they named the restaurant that," said Bert. They both looked at it in awe. "My, my!"

"You see," I whispered, elbowing Uncle Jack in the side. "Tourists like this place. It's different."

Miss Bowzer had come over to our table to say hello to me. I introduced her to Evie and Bert, who were very impressed to meet a real chef, I could tell.

"I saw a great recipe recently, air-dried beef and marinated lentils on radicchio, that I thought you might like to add to your menu, Miss Bowzer," said Uncle Jack.

"Nobody I know would order it, Mr. Dion," said Miss Bowzer, staring stonily at Uncle Jack.

"We're expecting a big tourist influx, Miss Bowzer," said Uncle Jack.

"I hope they like waffles," said Miss Bowzer.

All the adults turned their gaze suddenly as Miss Honeycut, who was dining out with her colleagues, approached our table. If looks could kill, there were four adults aiming right between her eyes.

"Hello, Primrose," said Miss Honeycut briskly. "Mr. Dion. Introduce me to your foster parents, Primrose." I guess she didn't say hello to Miss Bowzer because you don't talk to the help. I thought this was terrible but just the way she had been raised.

"We like to think of ourselves as just friends," said Evie. "I'm Evie and this here's Bert."

"Miss Honeycut," said Miss Honeycut, holding out her hand.

"I think it's a rotten thing you did, sending this child so far from home," said Evie, standing up and looking Miss Honeycut right in the midriff.

"Nonsense," said Miss Honeycut, not at all perturbed. "In the first place I didn't send her anywhere. The province is in charge of that. She can't go on leaving pieces of herself all over town: a finger here, a toe there. I remember when I went to school, my first boarding school, Mumfries, in Wales, actually . . ."

Miss Honeycut launched into one of her long anecdotes, this one about some cat who kept having accidents. "In the end there was so little left of her that the mouse was stalking her. *The mouse was stalking her.*"

We all sat silently while Miss Honeycut guffawed. She stopped suddenly, flushed, flared her nostrils, raised one eyebrow, and got all brisk again.

"Well, I was just going home. Goodbye, Primrose, Mr. Dion. Charming to have met you, Evie and Bert." She turned and left to join her friends, who were paying the bill.

Miss Bowzer looked daggers at her, shrugged, and returned to the kitchen.

Uncle Jack made a low sound in his throat, almost a growl.

"She's got a lot of stories, doesn't she?" I said.

The three of them looked at me in disbelief.

"We think it's terrible what they done, taking your niece from you," said Evie to Uncle Jack while we waited for our food and played with our ice water and sugar packets and stuff.

"Terrible thing," said Bert.

"Things are looking up," said Uncle Jack. "We're going to have this whole mess straightened out before long."

"Still, it's a terrible thing," said Evie as the food arrived. "And the poor tyke has to get used to a whole new school."

"Eh-hem," said Uncle Jack. He looked uncomfortable. He was using all his persuasive powers to try to get me home as swiftly as possible and I could see he was annoyed to be reminded that he hadn't had better luck.

"I like these waffles. They're good under lasagna, don't you think, Bert?" said Evie. "I'm going to try this at home."

I looked at Uncle Jack meaningly but he looked as if he had other things on his mind.

It sure was weird going to a motel with Evie and Bert and not to Uncle Jack's home with him.

Evie and Bert wanted to drive by and see my house.

"You ought to see it in the spring," I said. "My mother

isn't much of a gardener but she plants some shake-and-scatter seeds which grow a mix of long, tangled, old-fashioned flowers that are really beautiful until they wilt. My mother never bothers to pull out the dead flowers, so half the spring and summer the yard looks wonderful and the other half it looks terrible, but my mother says that it's all a question of how you want to spend your time and she likes to spend hers reading."

"Was your dad a gardener at all?" asked Evie as we sat parked in front of the house eating mints.

"No, he gets out and mows the lawn and rakes the leaves in a very businesslike way. And I think he likes to burn stuff. He burns stuff in a barrel every Friday. Sometimes I'd sit out with him and we'd just sit and watch things burn. We never talk much. He isn't much of a talker."

"Neither is Bert. Are you, Bert?" said Evie.

"Oh, I like a conversation," said Bert.

"You like a conversation, but you're not much of a talker. There's a difference," said Evie. "You don't talk *at* me but you'll talk *with* me. Right?"

"Right, Evie," said Bert.

The next morning Uncle Jack took Evie and Bert and me on a tour of all the new townhouses and condominiums that had gone up.

"Oh, Bert, it's so beautiful here," said Evie.

"It sure is, Evie," said Bert. "It reminds me of Nanaimo before the building boom."

"Are you thinking what I'm thinking?" said Evie.

That's how I ended up in Coal Harbour again. Of course, we went back to live in Nanaimo while Bert and Evie gave their house to a realtor to sell. Evie and Bert were so excited about moving for the first time in twenty-five years that I caught a little buzz from them and got all excited about our new town too, even though, technically speaking, it was my old town. Uncle Jack rented them a furnished unit until they sold their house and promised them the best deal he could on a townhouse in the same complex as Miss Honeycut. If he kept giving away places like this he was never going to make any money. Finally Evie and Bert pulled a rented trailer full of personal items up to Coal Harbour and we moved in. To celebrate, we went to The Girl on the Red Swing with Uncle Jack for pork chops (recipe to follow). We were just digging into our waffles when someone came running into the restaurant and yelled, "Fire!"

Cherry Pie Pork Chops

Preheat oven to 325 degrees. In a hot skillet (that same ovenproof one you used for your shepherd's pie) put a little oil and drop in your pork chops so that they sizzle and sear. Put some salt and pepper on them. Spoon 2 tablespoons of cherry pie filling on top of each chop and a little fruit juice on the bottom of the pan, say half an inch; pineapple is good. Cover the pan and bake for one hour. Take the chops out carefully so that the pie filling remains on top. Take some of the grease out of the pan, but not all of it, and add to the pan juices about a cup of sour cream. Put the sauce on the bottom of the plate and the chops on top of the sauce.

Miss Perfidy Leaves

Everyone looked around uncertainly for a second and then we heard the long mournful wail of the alarm, calling the volunteer fire department. Uncle Jack, like many able-bodied men in town, served as a firefighter and he leaped up and rushed out the door along with several other diners. The rest of us walked over to the windows to peer out and finally crowd outside to stand in a little huddle by the front door. You could smell smoke in the air and see flames down by the harbor.

Lots of people were rushing down Main Street.

"Can we go see?" I asked Evie.

"I don't know if we should go down there, do you, Bert?" asked Evie. "We might be in the way."

"I think it would be okay. From a distance," said Bert.

We might just as well because everyone else in the restaurant was. Even Miss Bowzer said she was going to lock up and go down and see what was burning and then return to unlock again so people could finish their dinners if they wanted to.

Evie and Bert and I were about the last ones down to the harbor because Evie couldn't walk very fast along those rutted roads in her high heels. There was quite a crowd gathered.

"Oh, my gosh," said Evie and her eyes looked even more surprised than usual. The townhouses were on fire. The whole complex had gone up like fireworks. "Quincehead! Quincehead!"

Bert ran after Evie, who tried to dash right into the inferno to find Quincehead. Luckily one of the firefighters stopped her and explained that they had rescued several pets already. Evie ran to where some people had volunteered to hold the frightened animals and she scooped Quincehead up and held him so tightly I thought she was going to suffocate him, which certainly would have been out of the fire and into the frying pan.

When we got over our joy at seeing Quincehead safe, we gazed in horror, realizing that all of Bert and Evie's photos and clothes and books and stuff were burning up, not to mention Uncle Jack's enterprise.

When I looked around for Uncle Jack, I found him hosing down the side of the complex with calm concentration just as if it were any other fire, and not racing in six directions at once yelling, "My townhouses! My townhouses!" which you or I might easily do.

The weight of its uselessness kept the crowd silent. The only sound came from the firefighters and the flames. Then over the sound of timbers collapsing came a scream.

"Someone's in there!" yelled a firefighter. "By you, Jack!"

Uncle Jack put down his hose.

"Oh, he can't go in there, Bert!" said Evie. "It's too dangerous."

"Someone's gotta go in," said Miss Bowzer, who was standing at my elbow.

"Be careful!" I yelled.

It seemed like a long time before we saw Uncle Jack again, so I was greatly relieved when we finally saw his jacket emerging from the door. Then I realized it wasn't Uncle Jack at all but a figure almost as tall but much thinner. A sudden burst of flames revealed that it was Miss Honeycut, who was being half supported and half pushed through the door by Uncle Jack, who had taken off his asbestos jacket and put it on her. Just as he came through it, the flaming door frame fell with a crash on his back. Miss Honeycut jumped out of harm's way and stood looking around wildly while the crowd yelled and a couple of nearby firefighters raced up to Uncle Jack. They put him in an ambulance and took him away with sirens screaming into the night louder than Miss Honeycut.

Bert and Evie and I went to Uncle Jack's house that night. I knew where the spare key was kept and I knew Uncle Jack would rather we stay there than go to a motel. Evie phoned the hospital and they told us not to bother coming down as we couldn't see Uncle Jack right now anyway. He was stabilized but unable to see visitors. I don't think any of us got much sleep. The phone kept ringing and the sheriff came and talked to Evie and Bert. The fire was out but smoke kept blowing all through the night. I wasn't going to settle down until I could see for myself that Uncle Jack was all right, so at dawn Evie and Bert and I drove down to Comox.

They had all kinds of bandages on Uncle Jack and the nurse said that burns were very painful but fortunately Uncle Jack's weren't very severe. Still, she said, between his burns and the ribs he had broken, he would need bed-rest for a little while. He smiled at us when we came in and there was a certain amount of teeth involved but I could see that even the corners of his mouth were weak.

"Do they know what caused the fire?" Uncle Jack asked Evie and Bert and that's when I noticed that Evie and Bert looked kind of shifty-eyed. They were so shifty-eyed that for a split second I had the crazy thought that *they* had set the townhouses on fire. Later in the car they explained that there was some talk that the wiring had been faulty.

"Could Uncle Jack get into trouble about that?" I asked. "He didn't build it. He just paid for it."

"Well, he could get into trouble if they prove that it was faulty because he didn't pay to have it done right and he paid off inspectors and things like that as some people are saying. Some developers would do that but not your uncle. It just don't make sense. I'm sure it will all be cleared up," said Bert.

"He don't know about it right now, Primrose. Even the sheriff can't believe your uncle would do that and the sheriff's not going to bother your uncle until he feels better," said Evie. "So we won't mention it either."

The next week we went to see Uncle Jack as often as we could. He didn't look good at all. And he looked worse once the sheriff told him that he had started an investigation into the cause of the fire and that it did look like it was caused by faulty wiring. Investors were pulling out. People were saying that Uncle Jack was the author of his own misfortune.

"You're not going to be sent to prison, are you?" I asked Uncle Jack nervously.

Uncle Jack looked up from his hospital bed where he was going through a stack of mail I had brought him. He grimaced every time he moved because of the pain in his ribs. "I hope not," he said simply, which was not reassuring.

Miss Honeycut had been released from the hospital the day after the fire. They had taken her in just as a precaution in case she had inhaled a lot of smoke. No one mentioned that she was only alive and unburned because of Uncle Jack. I guess it didn't occur to anyone that Uncle Jack could be a developer and a hero too. Instead of declaring that Uncle Jack had saved her life, Miss Honeycut turned around and tried to sue the pants off him because her valuables had burned up. And that's when I realized that my mother had been right all along about Miss Honeycut and I had been wrong. Miss Honeycut didn't tell anecdotes because she was interesting; she told them because she wasn't.

"Because," I said to Miss Bowzer later as I brought her up to date, "the only really interesting thing about someone that makes you want to explore them further is their heart, and Miss Honeycut has a teeny tiny pea-sized one and it takes you nowhere you want to go."

Miss Bowzer was teaching me to make Polynesian skewers (recipe to follow). We ended up absentmindedly eating a plate of them ourselves while Miss Bowzer got things ready for the early-bird crowd. She hadn't said a thing about Uncle Jack but I noticed that whenever I mentioned Miss Honeycut, she cut up the vegetables into small bits. BAM BAM BAM BAM BAM. The lunch rush was over and she looked frazzled and exhausted. When we had skewered our last bit of pineapple, she pulled up a stool and leaned her back against a counter, massaging her own shoulder. It was an awful lot of work for one person and I couldn't help thinking it was kind of sad that at best it would be a while again before all those tourists would be pouring into her restaurant, so that maybe she could afford some more help.

"I guess the world isn't going to be beating a path to your door now," I said.

She seemed surprised for a moment and then she looked dreamy-eyed around her big kitchen with its spills and dirty dishes and chaos from lunch preparation. But all she said was, "Judging by the mess, I'd say the world's already here."

Evie and Bert had recovered what they could from the fire. They said that they were sad about losing all their memory albums and stuff but that the insurance covered buying a new house. When Uncle Jack got out, they hoped he would help them find a nice mobile home someone wanted to sell.

"Do you think he finds those? Mobile homes aren't *real estate*, exactly, are they, Evie?"

"They're real estate that's *mobile*, Bert. It's real estate that *moves*," said Evie. "And the good thing, Primrose, is that now I can buy some more souvenirs. I had run out of room to put my souvenirs."

"Because we already had so many. When we travel, Evie likes to get souvenirs," said Bert.

"I like to get souvenirs but I had no *room* for them, so now I can start over. And I always wanted to macramé but I had no room for that either, unless I threw some already-displayed stuff out," said Evie.

"Which she didn't want to do on account of her sentiment," said Bert.

"I didn't want to do it but now I don't *have* to, thanks to that fire," said Evie.

"So there's always a bright side," said Bert.

Evie and Bert never got used to boys tripping through the house on their way to the gym. Each and every time, Evie would start and announce, "Burglars!" It was fortunate that Mallomar got on with Quincehead, but even so they had their days and then, after school, I would scoop up Mallomar and head down to the beach. Once on the way down I stopped at Miss Perfidy's on an impulse to see if we could dig up my sweaters.

"What's this? What's this?" she said, standing in the doorway pointing at Mallomar.

"That's Uncle Jack's dog," I said. "He's in the hospital, you know."

"Well, of course, I know that," said Miss Perfidy. "Everyone knows that. They say he set those buildings on fire himself. For the insurance."

"No, no," I said. "They don't say that, they say he *cheaped out* with the wiring and *that* caused the fire. But he didn't."

"Well, it's quite a year for you, isn't it?" she said, standing aside so that I could come in. "First your parents die, then your uncle Jack goes to jail."

"He's not in jail, he's in the hospital," I said patiently. "And my parents didn't die."

"Of course they died, don't be ridiculous," said Miss Perfidy. "Too many people indulging you in this notion. That's the problem."

I tried again. "There must be something you know, just know in your heart, Miss Perfidy. For no reason."

"There doesn't have to be any such thing, Primrose."

"Do you want me to put Mallomar in the backyard?"

"Do you think I'm afraid of dogs? After all the dogs I've had over the years?" Miss Perfidy snorted.

Miss Perfidy had never had a dog as long as I knew her but, to give her the benefit of the doubt, perhaps she had had some before I was born.

I followed her into the kitchen, where she was ironing a blouse.

"I ironed all these yesterday," she said, frowning and

picking up the iron. "But today when I came down, they all needed ironing again."

"You could think of it as a nice mystery," I suggested, but she glared at me. "Maybe you didn't iron them all yesterday. Maybe it was a false memory."

Miss Perfidy looked at me, irritably still, but there was a look in her eye that went from concerned to spooked a little too quickly. Her hair was even rattier than the last time I saw her and she was wearing shoes with no socks.

"Miss Perfidy," I said, not looking at her, "have you had any ideas about what might have happened to my sweaters because, you know, my mother knitted them all for me. And I'd like to have them."

"What are you worried about?" she continued irritably. "She can just knit you some more when she comes back, can't she? Isn't that what you keep saying, that she's coming back?"

"It's not that I don't think she's coming back," I began and then stopped because Miss Perfidy had stopped ironing and was standing with such a frozen expression I thought maybe she was going to have a heart attack or something. She put her hand to her mouth and worked her lips around worriedly between her fingers. Then she looked over at me. I stood up getting ready to call nine-one-one. She looked not quite there, or at least, even less there than usual and then she sat down on a kitchen chair and reached for a tea biscuit, so I knew she must be all right. I collapsed back on a chair. We sat there in silence for a moment because now she had me spooked. Then she got up abruptly, made herself a pot of tea, poured herself a cup, and sat down again to drink it.

"I think you had better go," she said. "I'm very tired."

"Are you okay?" I asked. "Because for a moment there—"

"For a moment there nothing," she snapped. "Here you come into my house telling me I can know things I don't know and see things that aren't there. If I told you my sister took your sweaters, you might ask me how I suddenly knew that, how I could see it in my mind's eye, just like that, but you're not going to, Primrose Squarp, because I won't be a party to such foolishness. Now, go on with you and not another word." She stood up and I picked up Mallomar.

"Is that what it was, then?" I asked. "Did you suddenly see something in your mind's eye?"

"It's all daydreams and thoughts you put in other people's heads. I don't plan to live to see the day I put stock in that." She squared her shoulders and marched me to the door, looking angry.

Miss Perfidy was right about not living to see the day.

The next day after school Evie and Bert and I drove down to visit Uncle Jack in the hospital and while we were in the hospital cafeteria grabbing a bite we ran into Mrs. Witherspoon sitting slumped at a table looking exhausted. She told us that Miss Perfidy had been taken ill in the middle of the night and was up in intensive care and not expected to live much longer. Mrs. Witherspoon had been crying and her eyeliner was smeared under her eyes. Evie made the right kind of clucking noises so that even though she was a stranger Mrs. Witherspoon rattled on to her.

"I knew she was failing, of course," said Mrs. Witherspoon. "I've been worried about her for some time and preparing to put her in a home. I would have had her move in with me but I'm not so young myself. Lately, every time I visited her I cleared some things out of her house for her. I tried to box things and take them out tactfully because she didn't like it. Sometimes I did it while she was out shopping. It seems mean but she had piles of old newspapers and magazines, boxes of canning jars—she hasn't canned in twenty years—old children's sweaters and used vacuum bags. She was saving her used vacuum bags. Can you get over that?"

"Did you take the children's sweaters out of a dresser upstairs?" I asked.

"Well, no," said Mrs. Witherspoon in some surprise. "But there was a box of them in the attic."

"Do you remember what they looked like?" I asked. "Was there a navy cardigan and a ski sweater with deer across the yoke?"

"Yes, I think so," said Mrs. Witherspoon. "They weren't yours, were they?"

I nodded.

"Oh, mercy," said Mrs. Witherspoon. "I'm so sorry. I thought it was just more accumulated junk. You know, sweaters kids had left behind when she baby-sat them years ago. I'm afraid I gave them to Goodwill."

"We'll go to Goodwill later and have a look," said Evie to me.

But I wasn't thinking about my sweaters, I was remembering Miss Perfidy seeing, in her mind's eye, her sister spiriting away my sweaters. I wanted to tell her that she had been right.

"Do you want to go up and see her?" Mrs. Witherspoon asked me suddenly, as if she had read my mind. Part of me did and part of me was afraid of intensive care. Evie and Bert tactfully said they thought they'd go back up to see Uncle Jack.

Intensive care was scary. There were lots of bodies on beds separated only by curtains and everyone was hooked into so many machines. It was quiet except for the raspy sound of respirators. Mrs. Witherspoon checked to see that Miss Perfidy was still okay. A nurse smiled compassionately at us and said "So far, so good" to Mrs. Witherspoon in a too-cheery voice that told us just how serious the situation was, and then she and Mrs. Witherspoon left Miss Perfidy's curtained area, saying they would leave me alone with her for a few minutes.

I sat next to Miss Perfidy's bed and looked at all the tubes in her nose and things taped to her and I didn't know what to say. Then, as I saw her sister coming back into intensive care, I thought I had better say something, so I said, "Well, Miss Perfidy, it's Primrose and I hear you're pretty sick and I wanted to tell you . . ." but I stopped there because suddenly a little alarm went off and nurses and doctors came in at a run with equipment, but what it turned out to be was that as I was standing there, Miss Perfidy had left the room in the middle of my sentence. Permanently.

"Oh, Miss Perfidy," I whispered to her as I was jostled aside by doctors and nurses trying to jolt her back to life with machines. "You knew things too. You just wouldn't believe that you knew them."

Polynesian Skewers

Take a slice of bacon and stick the end of it through a skewer. Then put a piece of pineapple on, then another bit of the bacon, then a water chestnut, piece of red pepper, mushroom, olive, or whatever vegetable or fruit is appealing. Grill until the bacon is done.

Everybody Goes Home

It was really sad after that. Mrs. Witherspoon was crying so hard that Evie and Bert decided to drive her home and we stayed with her while Evie made her a pot of tea and something to eat because she hadn't eaten all day. We all sat around the kitchen table while Mrs. Witherspoon ate scrambled eggs and reminisced about growing up with Miss Perfidy and Evie worked on her macramé and drank tea and Bert and I, I have to admit, pretty much just sat there. I thought how strange it was after a death when everyone is kind of stunned. Mrs. Witherspoon, I was sure, would never normally sit and eat eggs in front of a bunch of strangers without offering them anything too. And then when she was done with her eggs there was a long silence while we just watched Evie work on her macramé as though for all the world that's why we were there. Finally, Mrs. Witherspoon said to Evie, "What *is* that that you're doing?"

"Macramé," said Evie cheerfully. "I'm making a plant hanger to replace some things of ours that got burnt up in a fire. In the worst of times I find there's always something useful you can do with your hands." Then some other people started arriving to comfort Mrs. Witherspoon, so we said goodbye. It was early evening and a long drive back to Coal Harbour, but we stopped at Goodwill on the way out of town when we saw by the lights that they were still open to see if we could find any of my sweaters. None of them were there, which didn't surprise me. They were very nice sweaters. I hoped the children wearing them appreciated that they were hand-knit.

The week before Christmas, Uncle Jack got out of the hospital and he and I took long therapeutic walks on the beach. He was still in a lot of pain and walked very, very slowly but Mallomar and I didn't mind, we were so glad to have him back. Despite the pain, and the lawsuits, and his failing business, he was chipper.

"How can you stay so cheery?" I asked.

"Things are looking up," he said. "Electrician admitted to the sheriff today that he cut corners to make a bigger profit himself, so at least I'm cleared of *that*."

"Well, I guess that is good news," I said. "But your development project is kind of sunk, isn't it?"

"Oh, too early to tell, but if it is, you know it wouldn't be the first time, Primrose." He picked up a rock and skipped it across the water. It skipped seven times. He was an amazing stone-skipper. The most I had ever gotten was four.

The gray winter surf was barreling in. The waves crashed and the wind tangled my hair and roared in my ears.

Mallomar had stopped chasing birds for the last few weeks. She was an older and wiser puppy and knew she couldn't catch them. That's why it surprised me when suddenly off she went—as though she had been shot out of a cannon, flying down the beach, her feet barely visible on the sand. Over logs she dove, through surf, changing direction in a split second in midair.

"Why does she do that?" I asked Uncle Jack as we watched her in admiration. "She knows she can't catch them."

"Just for the sheer joy of the motion," said Uncle Jack.

Then we waved to Evie and Bert, who were hobbling over the boulders, tripping down to us on the beach.

"Halloo! Halloo!" they called.

Uncle Jack had sent them off to walk by a likely-looking mobile home he was selling. He said he thought he could get them a deal.

"It's a charmer," said Bert as they came panting up to us, all excited. "It's bigger than I thought it would be."

"It's big but it's not *too* big," said Evie, "so that we can drive it comfortably down to Arizona—when your uncle Jack gets custody again of you, which we all know he's going to do, as soon as Miss Honeycut drops her lawsuit."

"Or is proven wrong in a court of law," said Bert.

"Or is proven wrong in a court of law . . . speak of the devil . . ." said Evie, and we all looked because Miss Honeycut was walking down the waterfront road carrying shopping bags. School would let out soon and Miss Honeycut would be leaving to spend her usual two weeks in Europe. As we looked, she bumped right smack into Miss Bowzer, who was hustling down the street, turning the corner without looking, an industrial-sized can of mustard in her arms.

There was a moment of confusion while they bumped heads. Sheriff Peters was ambling by and he bent over and picked up and handed the packages to Miss Honeycut, who was frowning and didn't even seem to say thank you, and then Miss Bowzer spied us and waved. I can still see the whole scene detail by detail because of what happened next.

A boat chugged by and started heading in for the main pier and we all turned to look. It wasn't a fishing boat and we couldn't imagine what kind of fool would take a pleasure boat out on such wild waters, but the people on the deck were standing against the rail looking excitedly to shore as if for all the world they were on a cruise. And I saw that it was my parents and at the same time saw everyone's reaction as if I were filming it all in slow motion. Miss Bowzer dropped the cigarette right out of her mouth, Miss Honeycut looked horrified as if she had made some terrible mistake and didn't know what to do about it, Evie and Bert were looking at me because I was making gakking noises, and Uncle Jack simply rolled his eyes back and fainted dead away on the sand. Well, he was still pretty ill. I looked down at him in astonishment as the sheriff ran over to us. Sheriff Peters was cool as a cucumber, as always, and immediately began first aid. Miss Bowzer dashed over next and held Uncle Jack's head up out of the muck, saying to me, "The sheriff and I have him, go on, go on!" So I flew across the sand but as I was running I was thinking that all along I had thought Uncle Jack believed as I did that my parents were still alive because he never ever once contradicted me but now I knew that all along he had been certain they were dead and, as happy as I was to see my parents again, the most prominent emotion I had at that moment was just overwhelming gratitude because he had stood at my side all those months keeping the faith even when he didn't believe it himself.

My parents ended up in the Comox Hospital because they were emaciated and needed to be checked out. During that first week we all told our stories and I showed them my missing digits. My mother said that when she had set out in our skiff she really had no hope of finding my father but she pushed on and on into the storm. She came upon his boat finally. It was taking on a lot of water from both sides and he was just inflating the dinghy when he spied her. She tried to bring her boat into his but collided against the side and fell overboard. My father threw the dinghy with two survival suits into the water and abandoned the fishing boat. He managed to finally get my mother on board the dinghy, help her get her raincoat off, which blew over the side, and put her survival suit on her, but she had gotten wet enough that he was worried about hypothermia. Finally they were flung, he said, almost airborne through the waves until they crashed against some rocks on an island. It wrecked the dinghy but they were alive and they crept onto land where they had lived very much like Robinson Crusoe all this time. They were disoriented by the storm, so my father wasn't exactly sure where they were but he knew they couldn't be that far out of the range of small craft that might sail in close enough to spot them, so they took turns all this time watching. They were finally spotted by the couple who rescued them, who had rented a boat to look for grizzly bears. At first they thought my parents were grizzly bears and motored in to get a closer look and were surprised to see two gaunt, savage-looking people.

"But now you're home!" said Evie. "Does anyone want a mint?"

"Oh, how lovely, mints!" said my mother and then my parents had to go off and rest and Uncle Jack and Evie and Bert and I drove back home, where Uncle Jack was relocating the couple who had rented our house to another house for free, although they said they would have moved anyway. My parents were a seventh-day wonder in Coal Harbour that week.

I ran into Miss Honeycut on the street the day after my parents got out of the hospital. She immediately started speaking six to the dozen.

"So, I guess you're happy your parents are home again. Quite an amazing thing. I'm happy for you, Primrose. I imagine you're feeling very grateful."

I was, not just for their return but for their absence too, and where it had taken me and who I had met there. I would never go home again in quite the same way, but that was okay too.

I was feeling so grateful that I expansively invited Miss Honeycut to join us that evening at The Girl on the Red Swing. My parents were taking Evie and Bert and Uncle Jack and me to dinner to celebrate and somehow I suddenly felt sorry for Miss Honeycut, who was always so alone. She jabbered on as usual, but this time I made myself pay attention.

"Thank you very much but I'm afraid I'm unable to make it. You see I'm flying out of Coal Harbour tonight. I got the unfortunate news yesterday that my father has passed away at last and so, of course, I plan to return to England as I have always planned to do, to take over the manor house and attend to things. First I shall see my father's many friends around Europe, which I quite prefer to having them all attend a funeral. No, it will be a small private funeral and I shall spend the winter months in Capri visiting the godparents and Father's good friends in Paris, and then on to Germany and Austria for the cousins, after that to Denmark and Amsterdam because there are some exhibitions I wish to see. Do you know Vermeer?"

"No," I said.

"Pity," she said. "Well, I shan't be returning to Coal Harbour." And then she did something odd. She reached down and grabbed my hand and shook it briefly, a cold, hard, lifeless shake, and turned around and I never saw her again.

All my life I had wanted to travel but what I discovered that year was that the things that you find out become the places that you go and sometimes you find them out by being jettisoned off alone and other times it is the people who choose to stand by your side who give you the clues. But the important things that happen to you will happen to you even in the smallest places, like Coal Harbour. I thought of Lena and her potatoes and wondered whether if she had sat tight, they would have happened to her here too. Years later my mother got a Christmas card from Lena saying that she was divorced now and practicing law—that James was still a genius and that Ryan was a handful but she had him in therapy—and thanking my mother for her help that day. She added that she had gotten the blue ribbon for the best boiled potatoes. No one, she said, had ever asked her how she had done in the contest.

So I stopped envying Miss Honeycut, who traveled so many places with eyes wide shut, and hoped someday she would look next to her and find someone to whom she could bear to listen.

We never any of us heard from her again although her friends kept expecting an invitation to the manor house, even two years after her departure. She left so quickly she had one of her friends at the school tidy up her Coal Harbour affairs and ship what she wanted and sell the rest. After that, the friend never got a postcard from her, much less an invitation. No, we all disappeared clean out of her mind, or perhaps not; perhaps we became anecdotes on the other side of the ocean.

That night, as planned, we all went for dinner at The Girl on the Red Swing. We asked Miss Bowzer to join us. She couldn't because she was busy cooking but she came in right before we ordered, opened Uncle Jack's menu for him, and stabbed a finger at it, pointing to something. Uncle Jack, startled, looked down to see where she was pointing and then a long smile spread across his face. Of all the smiles I had seen on Uncle Jack's face, this was the best.

"Why, Miss Bowzer. I'll be a monkey's uncle," he said, which was pretty inadequate and goes to show how rattled he was. But Miss Bowzer seemed satisfied. She smiled and turned on her heel to head back to the kitchen. We all flipped through our menus surreptitiously to see what she had pointed to, while Uncle Jack beamed into his, unaware of us apparently. I was the only one who knew what it was when I saw it. It was a new item: air-dried beef and marinated lentils on a bed of radicchio. Uncle Jack ordered it and it wasn't until he had eaten halfway through it that he saw the waffle underneath.

And it was always like that in Coal Harbour. Some people got old and some died. I left parts of myself some places and found others unexpectedly. New people appeared on the scene and others disappeared before I had a chance to say goodbye. All kinds of ordinary people gave their whole hearts to things you wouldn't think you could give your heart to. I made discoveries like the reason for Miss Honeycut's anecdotes, and other things, like the whereabouts of my sweaters, remained a mystery forever. And Coal Harbour never became a big resort or swank tourist spot or anything, but I didn't care because I knew that as long as you lived there you could get anything you wanted. And it always came on a waffle. (Recipe to follow.)

Waffles

Mix together 2 cups of flour, 1 tablespoon baking powder, 2 tablespoons sugar, ½ teaspoon salt. In another bowl put 3 large and well-beaten eggs, ½ stick of butter, and 1½ cups of milk. Make a hole in the middle of your dry ingredients and pour in the wet ingredients and stir it all up. Make sure your waffle iron is hot and greased if it is the type that is supposed to be greased and then pour in enough batter so that it spreads all over but not quite to the edge or it will end up leaking out the sides and making a big mess. If you have an electric waffle iron, it will tell you when the waffles are done, otherwise you must check them and turn the iron on the burner until the waffle is brown. Serve with butter and syrup. Or if you are at The Girl on the Red Swing, everything.